LEONARDO

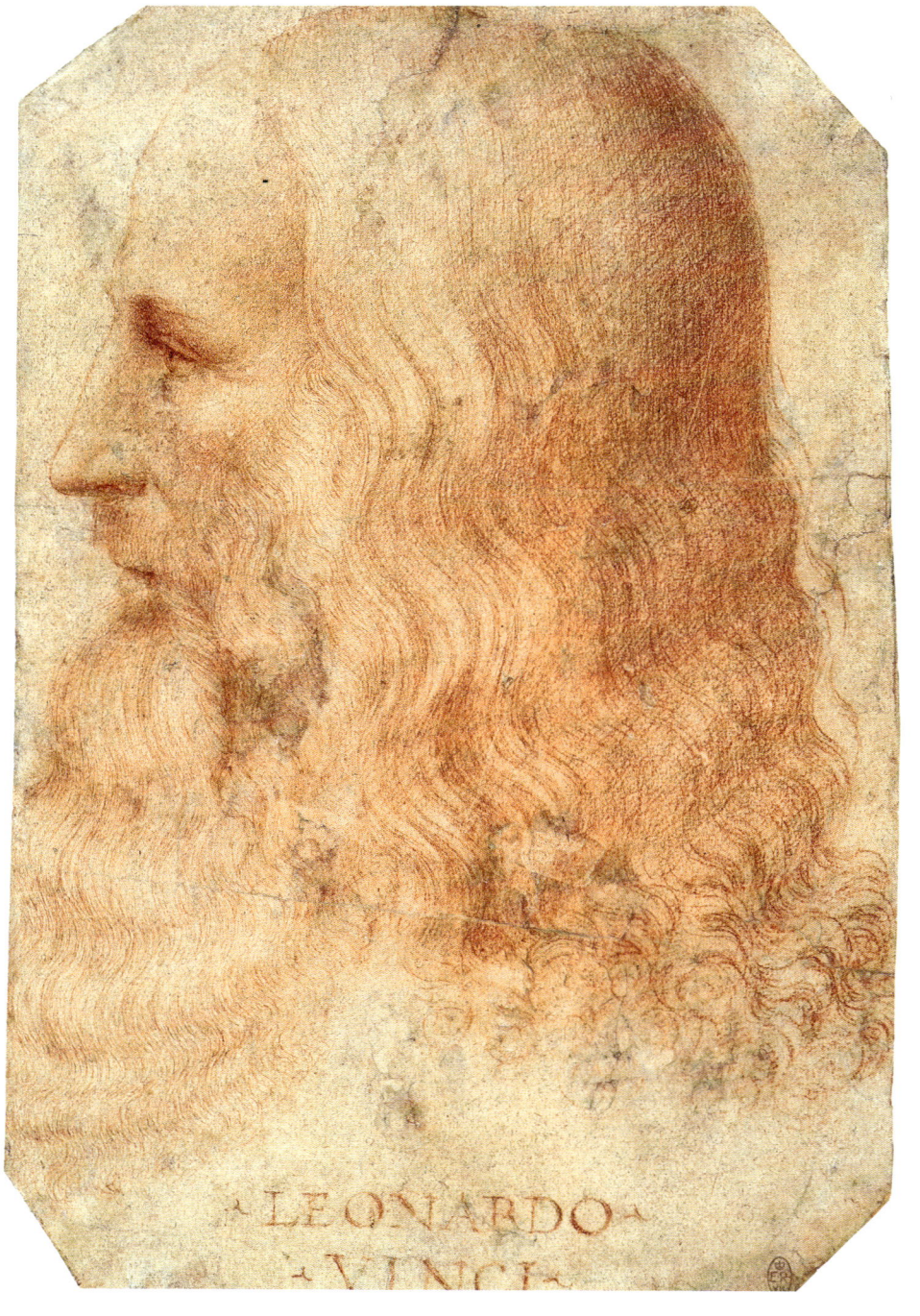

·LEONARDO·
·VINCI·

MASTERS OF ART

LEONARDO

Alexander Adams

PRESTEL

Munich · London · New York

Front Cover: Leonardo da Vinci, *Cecilia Gallerani (Lady with an Ermine)*, c. 1489–90,
(see page 64)
Frontispiece: Attributed to Francesco Melzi, *Portrait of Leonardo da Vinci*,
c. 1512–3? or c. 1519
pages 8/9: Head of a Bearded Man (Self-portrait?), c. 1510–5 (see page 103)
pages 38/39: Annunciation, c. 1473–5? (see page 49)

© Prestel Verlag, Munich · London · New York 2025
A member of Penguin Random House Verlagsgruppe GmbH
Neumarkter Strasse 28 · 81673 Munich

1st edition 2025

produktsicherheit@penguinrandomhouse.de
(The above information is mandatory information according to GPSR and should be
used for all queries relating to the safety of our books)

A CIP catalogue record for this book is available from the British Library.

Editorial direction: Anja Besserer
Picture editing: Fiona Krech
Copyediting and proofreading: Vanessa Magson–Mann, So to Speak, Icking
Production management: Michael Graupner
Design: Florian Frohnholzer, Sofarobotnik
Typesetting: Uhl + Massopust, Aalen
Separations: Reproline mediateam
Printing and binding: Longo AG
Typeface: Cera Pro

MIX
Paper | Supporting
responsible forestry
FSC® C023164

Penguin Random House Verlagsgruppe FSC® N001967
Printed in Italy
ISBN 978-3-7913-9161-8
www.prestel.com

CONTENTS

INTRODUCTION

What can one say about Leonardo da Vinci (1452–1519), the artist who for us defines the Italian Renaissance? Thousands of books, articles and catalogue entries describe the achievements of this great artist and pioneering scientist. This book can only touch upon bare facts and major art works, but in truth very little definitively established will be left out. For an individual who bequeathed to us a wealth of information in thousands of manuscript pages—one of the glories of Western civilisation—Leonardo wrote little about himself. The Leonardo you know is partly assumed and deduced, not recorded by him or those who personally knew him.

In a short book about his art, we must almost entirely pass over Leonardo's formidable accomplishments in the fields of—among others—anatomy, biology, hydrodynamics and hydraulics, engineering, flight, optics and weaponry. The embodiment of Renaissance-man-as-polymath, Leonardo straddles the Italian Early and High Renaissance, respectively defined as roughly 1453–1490 and 1490–1520. This was a time when artists were trained to be able to turn their hands to disparate activities. They were often painters, print designers, metalsmiths and sculptors, in addition to being engineers and architects. Serving the Church, states, princes and dukes—not to mention private patrons—they also designed costumes and sets for theatrical performances, parades and state occasions. We know that Leonardo did all this, as well as making everything from flying machines to ingenious mechanical toys.

This introduction could be filled with the bare descriptions of Leonardo's various activities. He was wonderfully adaptable, curious and resourceful. This was to his patrons' advantage, but to our disadvantage (as art lovers). There is no doubt that Leonardo would have produced more paintings, drawings and sculptures had he not been occupied with scientific enquiry, engineering tasks and satisfying the contingent demands of his patrons. Yet it is undeniable that he went beyond what was necessary or expected in those areas. Leonardo was liable to be distracted and detained due to his insatiable curiosity and perfectionism. He was not well adapted to do the one thing we would most love for him to have done: to shut himself in a studio and—to the exclusion of all else—make art.

Leonardo is the most reticent and reluctant painter of all the great masters. No important artist painted as infrequently as he did. He painted slowly and little; he was the least artistically productive of all the major Renaissance masters. He left much of his work unfinished, becoming embroiled in legal cases with patrons disappointed by his tardiness. His painting was routinely delegated to assistants and trusted collaborators. Barely fifteen surviving paintings are confidently ascribed to Leonardo's hand, solely or principally. Attrition has removed a number of other pictures by him. While I am not persuaded by arguments in favour of the authenticity of two recently attributed works, I have included them in this book because they merit detailed discussion. The record of Leonardo's accomplishments in sculpture is even more scant, with no projects completed and not even a statuette today confidently ascribed to him.

The complexity of Leonardo's working practices, his close collaboration with assistants and the difficulty of dating many of his paintings and drawings makes examining his art confusing. This book keeps to a minimum idle speculation and elaborate theories, without glossing the difficulties. We must rely on copies and variants by followers to glimpse lost and unfinished pictures. Unfortunately, most of Leonardo's disciples are generally of low quality. Art historian Bernard Berenson dismissed art by Leonardo's followers, stating "most of these productions are of small intrinsic value. The only serious interest attached to them is that they record ideas of the master's.... Take away Leonardo's share in these compositions, and you have taken away nearly all that gave them worth". A harsh but largely accurate assessment.

It is in the codices (manuscript books) of drawings that we find the core genius of Leonardo. Perhaps three quarters of his working papers have been destroyed, which is a grievous loss. The drawings are lively, rich, sometimes breathtakingly exquisite. At times, Leonardo's mind is moving so fast his pen dashes to catch up. His essence lives on in pages of drawings, interspersed by notes, often in the form of questions that stray into profound areas of existence, probing the core of natural processes. Leonardo questions everything and demands to observe all first hand, which is the mark of his rigorous intellect and penetrating gaze.

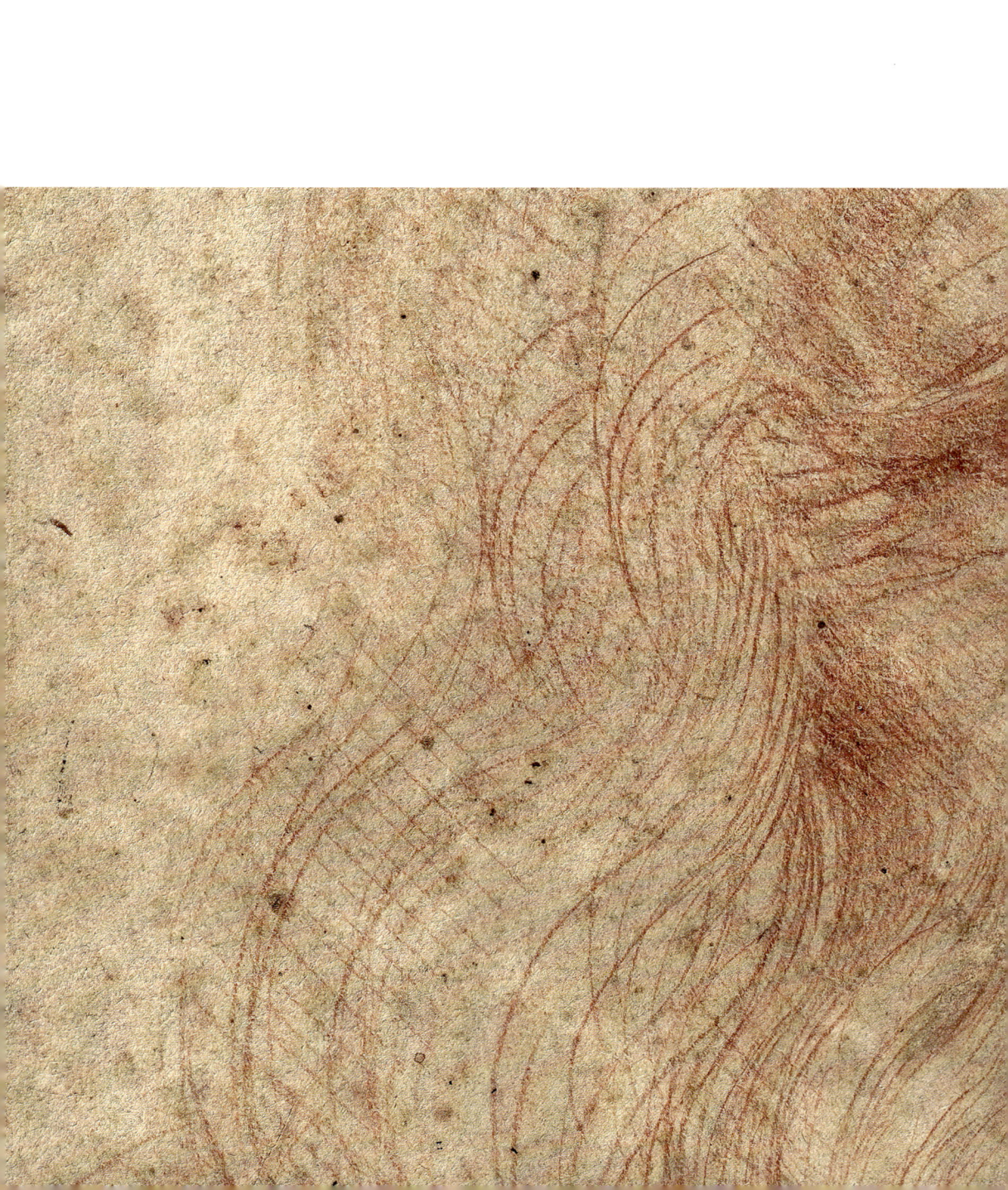

LIFE

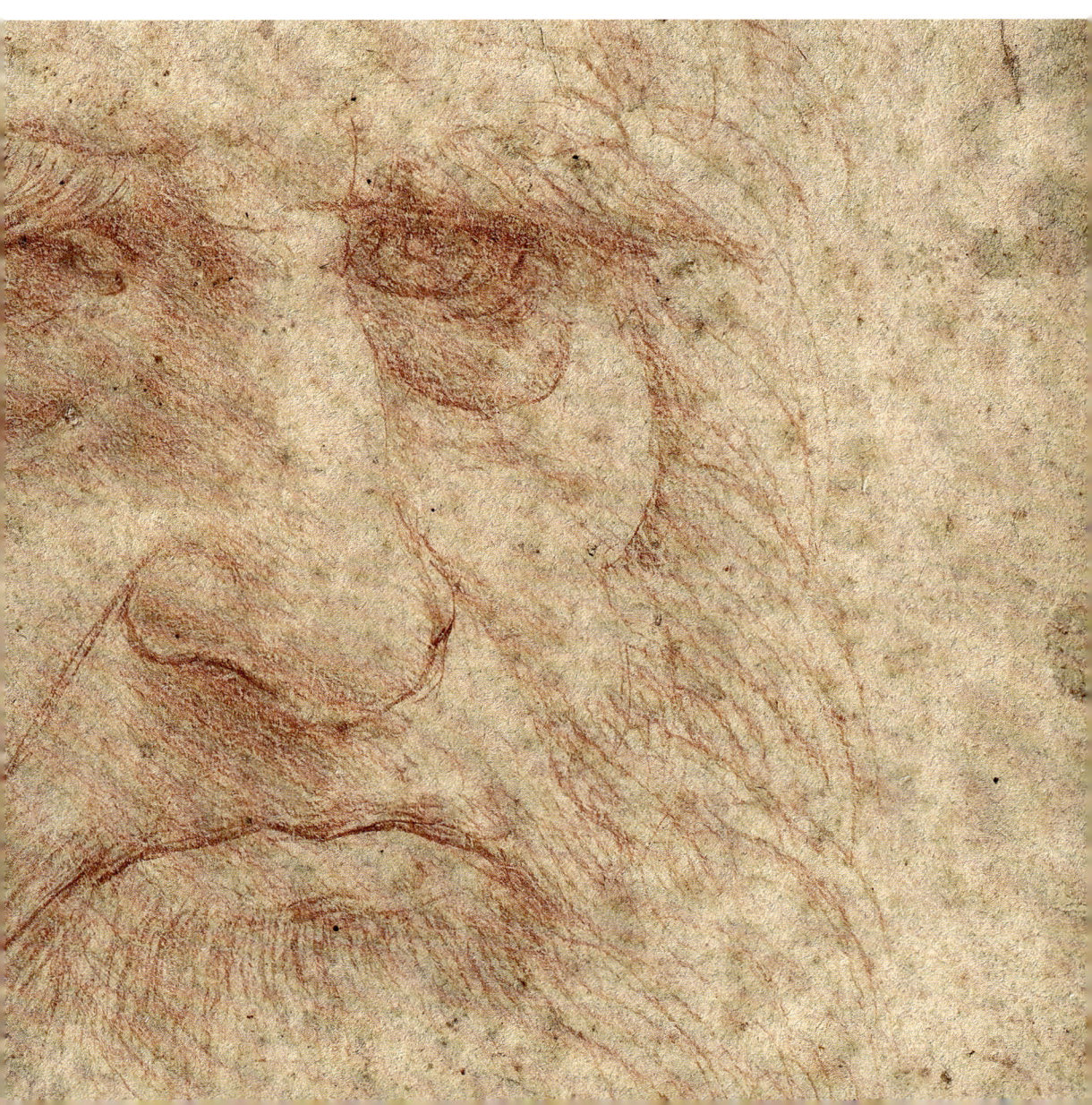

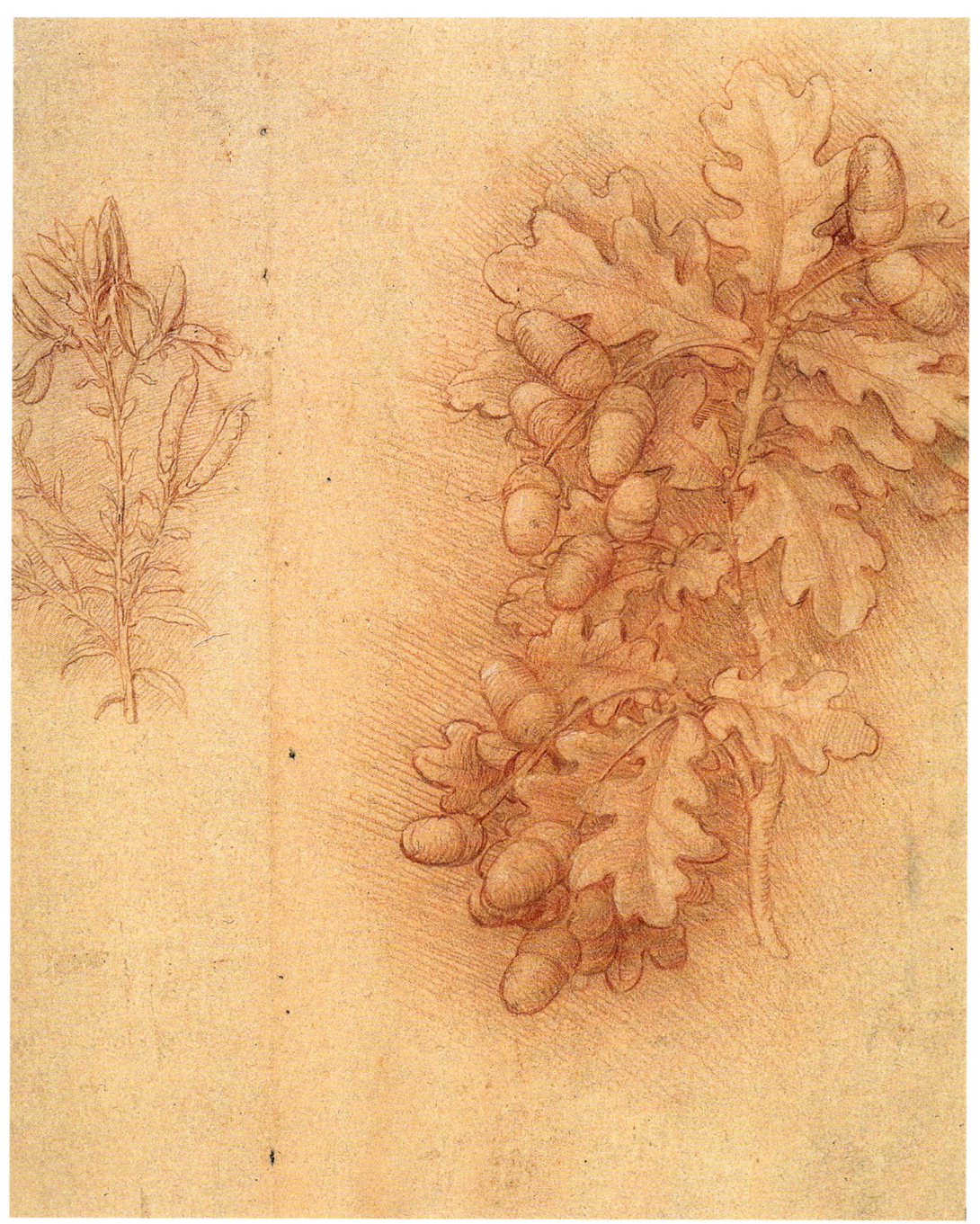

Leonardo di Ser Piero da Vinci was born on 15 April 1452, possibly in the hamlet of Anchiano, near Vinci, a village in the region of Florence. He was the illegitimate first-born son of Ser Piero da Vinci (1426–1504), a notary, and Caterina di Meo Lippi (c. 1427–1494/5?), a servant. Soon after he was born, Leonardo's mother married Antonio di Piero Buti del Vacca (called "Accattabriga"; c. 1425/30– c. 1490) a furnace worker. It seems that the infant Leonardo lived with his mother and step-father at a farm near Vinci before moving to his father's house. Ser Piero resided mainly in Florence, his place of work, later with a young wife (Leonardo's step-mother). Leonardo would eventually have many half-siblings (all younger) on both sides of his family. He was close to grandfather, Antonio (1393–1469) and paternal uncle, Francesco (1436–1507)—the latter would leave his nephew a legacy—and would spend much of his childhood in their homes.

Being illegitimate, Leonardo was unable to follow his father's profession. This may have contributed to his father's decision to give the child an education limited to literacy and numeracy. He was not taught languages (beyond the rudiments) and his natural left-handedness was never corrected. His country upbringing and lack of book-learning inculcated in the curious child a propensity to observe, experiment and remember. Unshackled by conventional wisdom, he was free of assumption and therefore lacked self-satisfied rigidity. Leonardo later commented, "All our knowledge has its foundation in our sensations. All science will be vain and full of errors which is not born of experience."

When Leonardo moved to Florence around 1466, he arrived as a youth without great education but nevertheless cultured. Ser Piero would have told his son about his distinguished clients. It was unlikely that this was the first time Leonardo had experienced the heady environment of Florence, a thriving centre of trade and culture under the rulership of Lorenzo de' Medici. It was the site of Brunelleschi's famed cathedral dome, one of the architectural marvels of Europe and a subject of wonder and pride for Florentines. At around 14 years' old, Leonardo was at the normal age for apprenticeship. Ser Piero knew artist Verrocchio in a professional capacity and arranged to have his son train under him. Ser Piero would have paid the fees required. For the first years of apprenticeship, masters were paid by their pupils' families; only when apprentices became experienced enough to perform to a high level were they themselves paid.

Andrea del Verrocchio (c. 1435–1488) trained—and collaborated with—many highly regarded Florentine artists of the periods we now call the Early and High Renaissance: Sandro Botticelli, Pietro Perugino, Domenico Ghirlandaio, Filippino Lippi, Luca Signorelli. He had been trained as a metalsmith and became a sculptor of great distinction. As a painter, Verrocchio was adequate and could provide pupils with a capable grounding in tempera painting. We shall discuss Leonardo's progress in painting later.

Leonardo absorbed the treatises of Leon Battista Alberti (1404–1472) and scrutinised the Baptistry doors of Lorenzo Ghiberti (1378–1455), as well as the new art of his time. Before learning

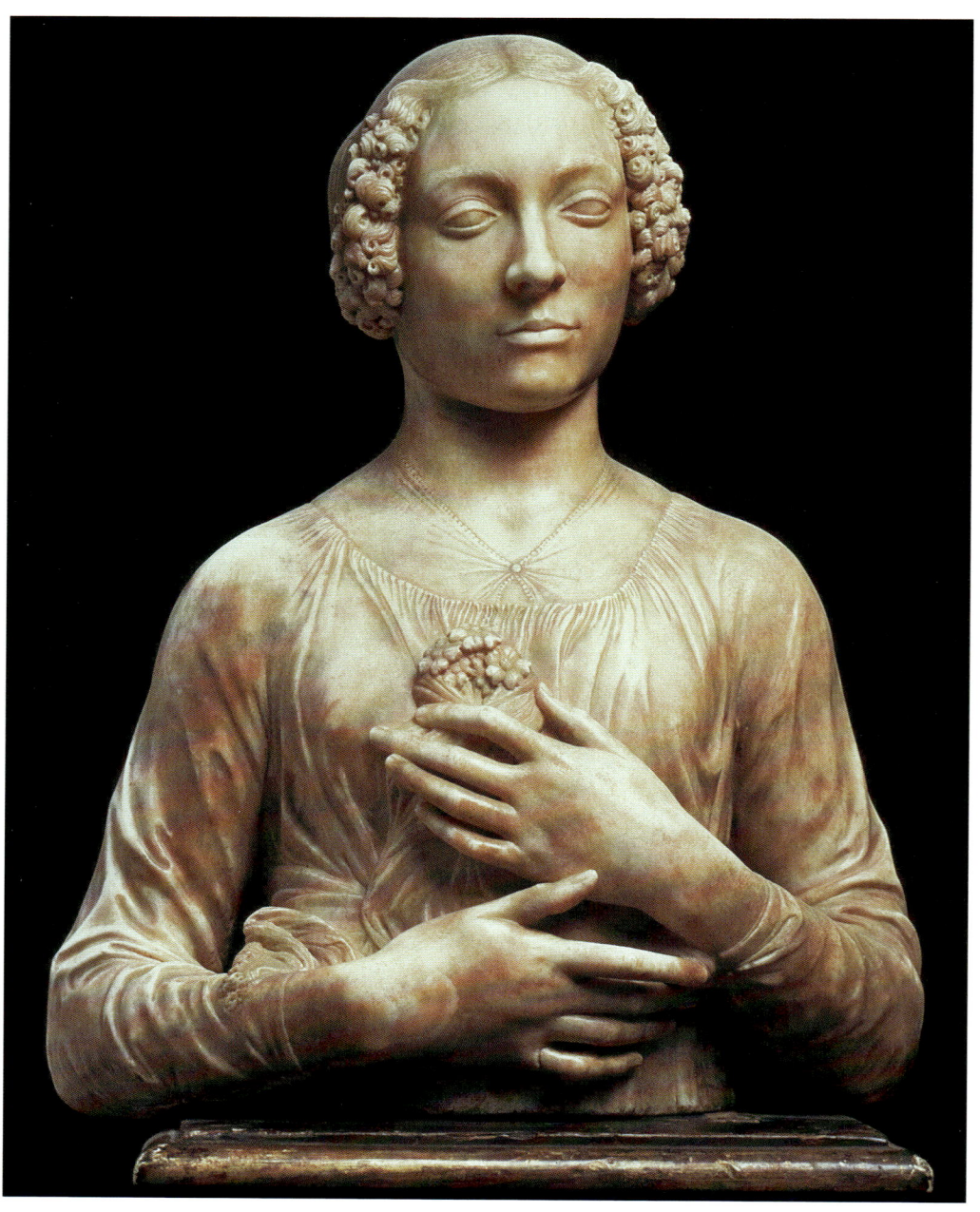

Andrea del Verrocchio, *Lady with Flowers*, 1475–80

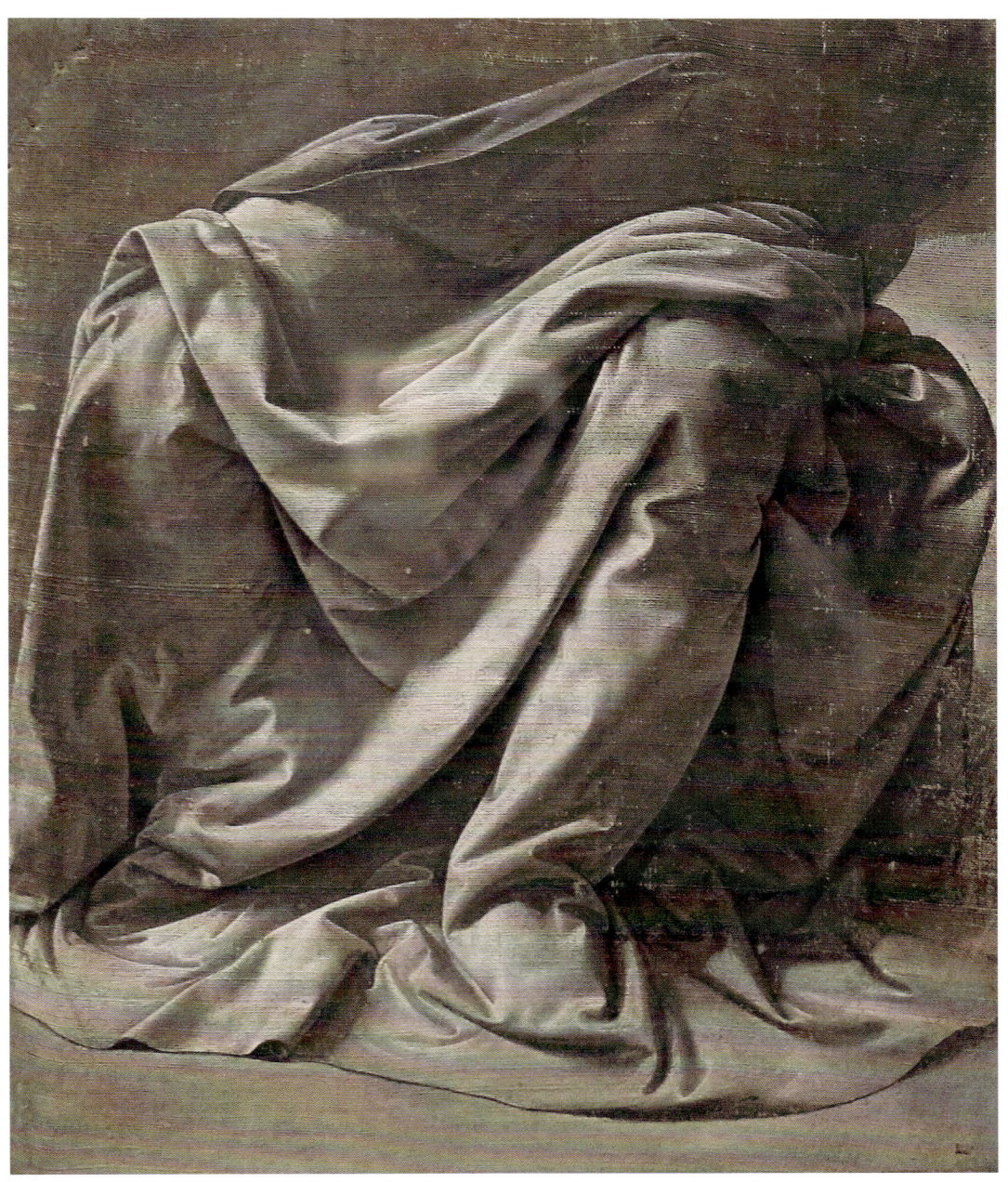

Drapery Study for a Seated Figure, c. 1475–82?

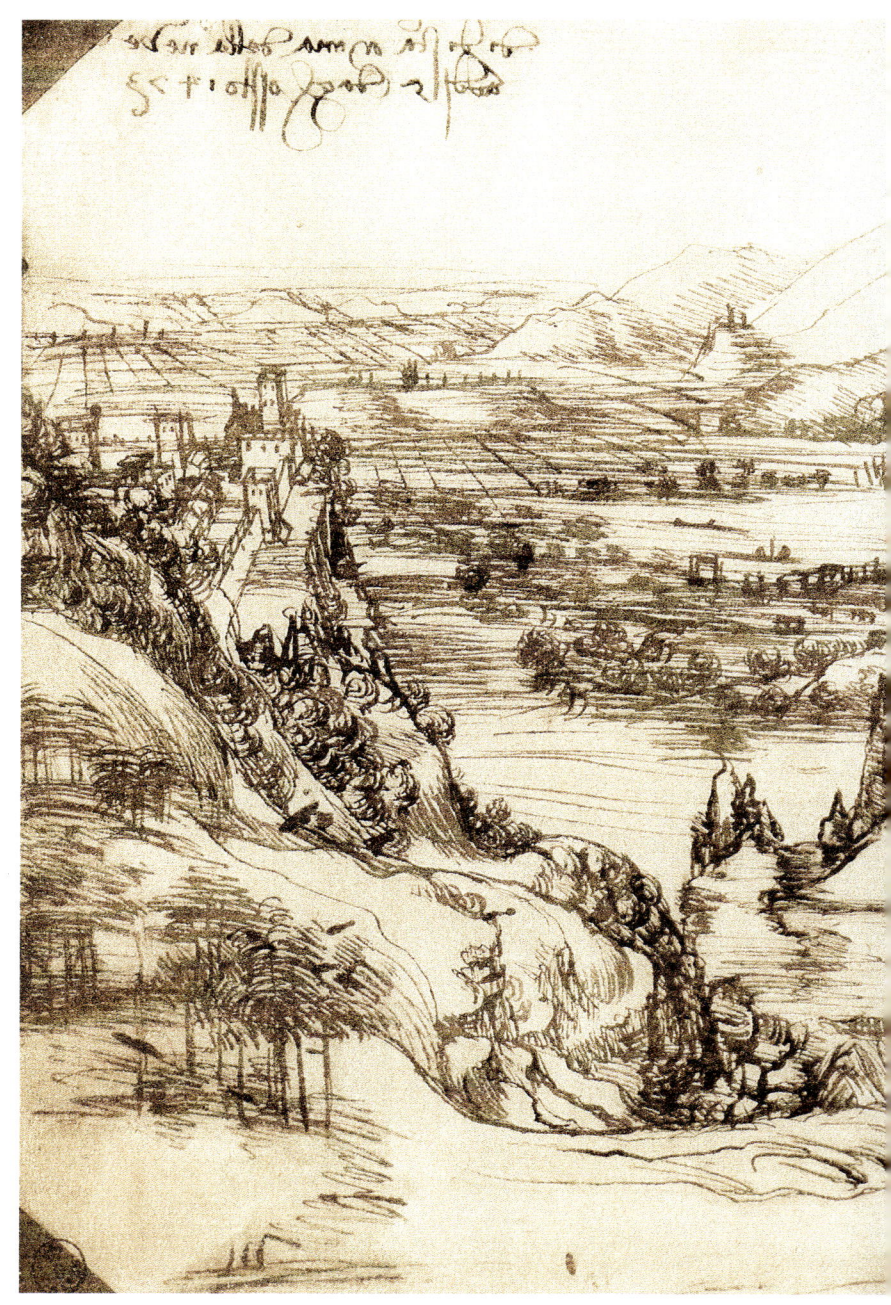

Arno Landscape, 1473

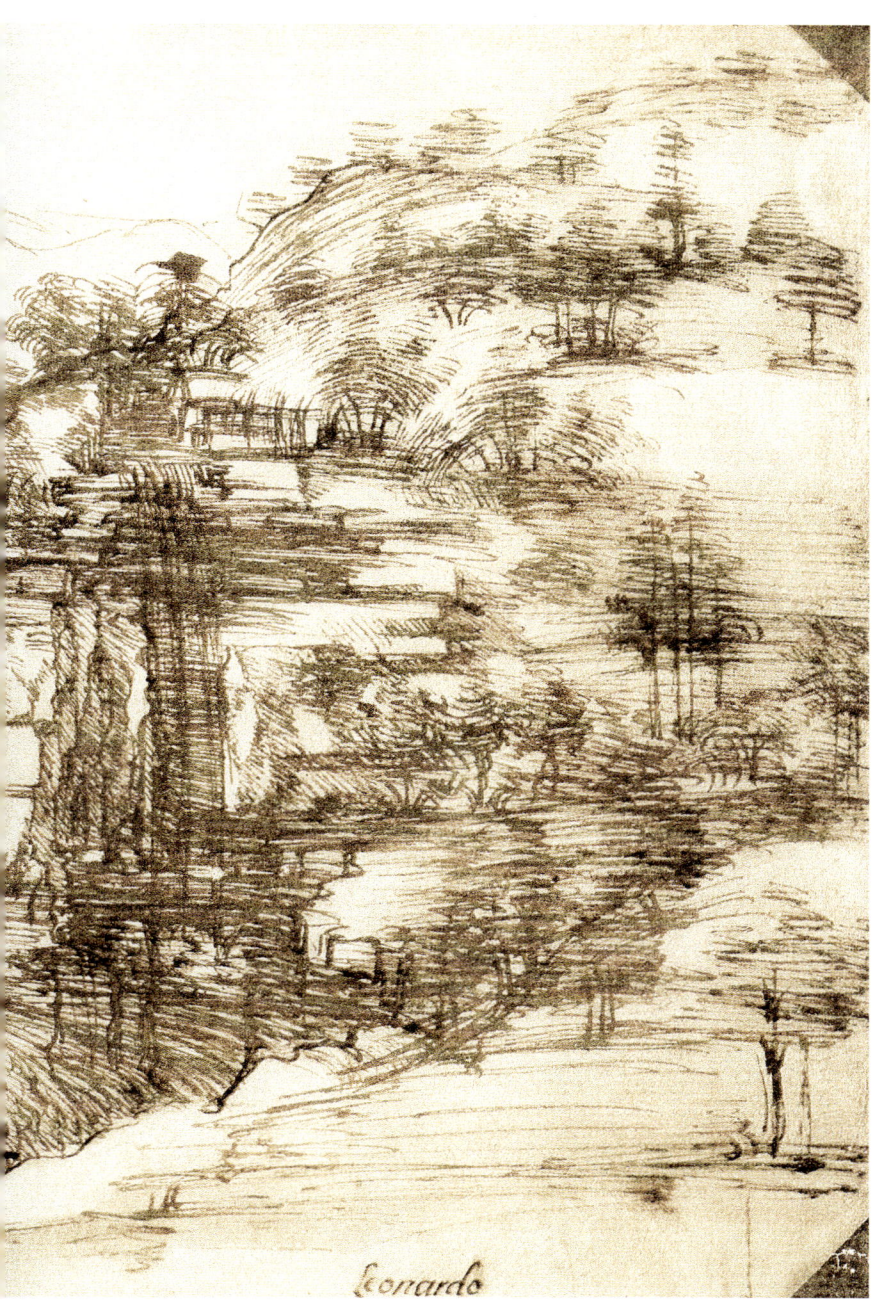

painting techniques, pupils were instructed in drawing. Leonardo learnt to draw in chalk and metalpoint (page 60); it is from this period we have detailed studies of drapery, following Verrocchio's technique (page 13). He was also taught how to prepare projects by testing designs in small compositional drawings, studying the effects of light, then making larger versions and detailed drawings of individual heads, hands and drapery. Full-size cartoons were used to transfer designs to painting supports (page 82). Leonardo would draw people, places, landscapes, plants and animals for pleasure. A page of cat sketches includes some that look like lions; a dragon is imagined in a feline pose (page 35). Colour was rarely tested in advance, as the Florentine method relied on drawing taking primacy, with colour playing a tertiary role, subordinated to the secondary role of shading.

On a visit to Vinci, Leonardo drew a landscape view. Inscribed "5 August 1473", it is considered the first dated drawing made outside in the open (pages 14/5). This may not be the case. Historians are attached to having a datable starting point of a practice later to become common, yet it seems this drawing is not an actual view made in situ but a composed fantasy. Leonardo did draw views and studies of plants *en plein air*, but this dated landscape lacks the documentary veracity we crave.

Leonardo assisted Verrocchio's workshop to forge and affix a gilded copper orb upon Brunelleschi's dome in 1471. He looked after the scaffold and winch constructed to hoist the orb, which weighed two tons. For architects or sculptors such engineering know-how was essential, as designers planned and oversaw construction of necessary machines, scaffolds and forges.

Leonardo developed quickly as a man too. He became an accomplished lute player and fine singer; at this time he cultivated sartorial elegance in his well-dressed Florentine milieu. Accounts note Leonardo as graceful and fastidiously clean, as well as handsome. As pupils were expected to, he modelled for colleagues. It is surmised Verrocchio's sculpture *David* (1473–5) is based upon the youthful Leonardo.

When Verrocchio learnt to paint, tempera was the almost universal painting medium in Italy. Tempera, wherein pigment is mixed with egg yolk, is durable but cannot be blended, as it dries fast. Shading is done in graduated bands and by minute hatching. Painting with linseed or walnut oil—which allows slow drying and smooth blending, as well as the concoction of semi-transparent glazes—began to spread in the 1460s. Pioneered by Netherlandish artists, the method was taken up by Antonello da Messina (1429/30–1479) and the Bellini brothers and was soon adopted widely. Leonardo was taught tempera painting but would choose to use oil paint for the leftmost angel in *The Baptism of Christ* (c. 1470–2 and c. 1475) (page 43). The delicacy, vibrance and verisimilitude of Leonardo's contribution marked him out as the best painter in the studio. He likely became Verrocchio's lead painter, later succeeded by Lorenzo di Credi (c. 1456/9–1537)—a weak painter but competent manager—with whom Leonardo would collaborate.

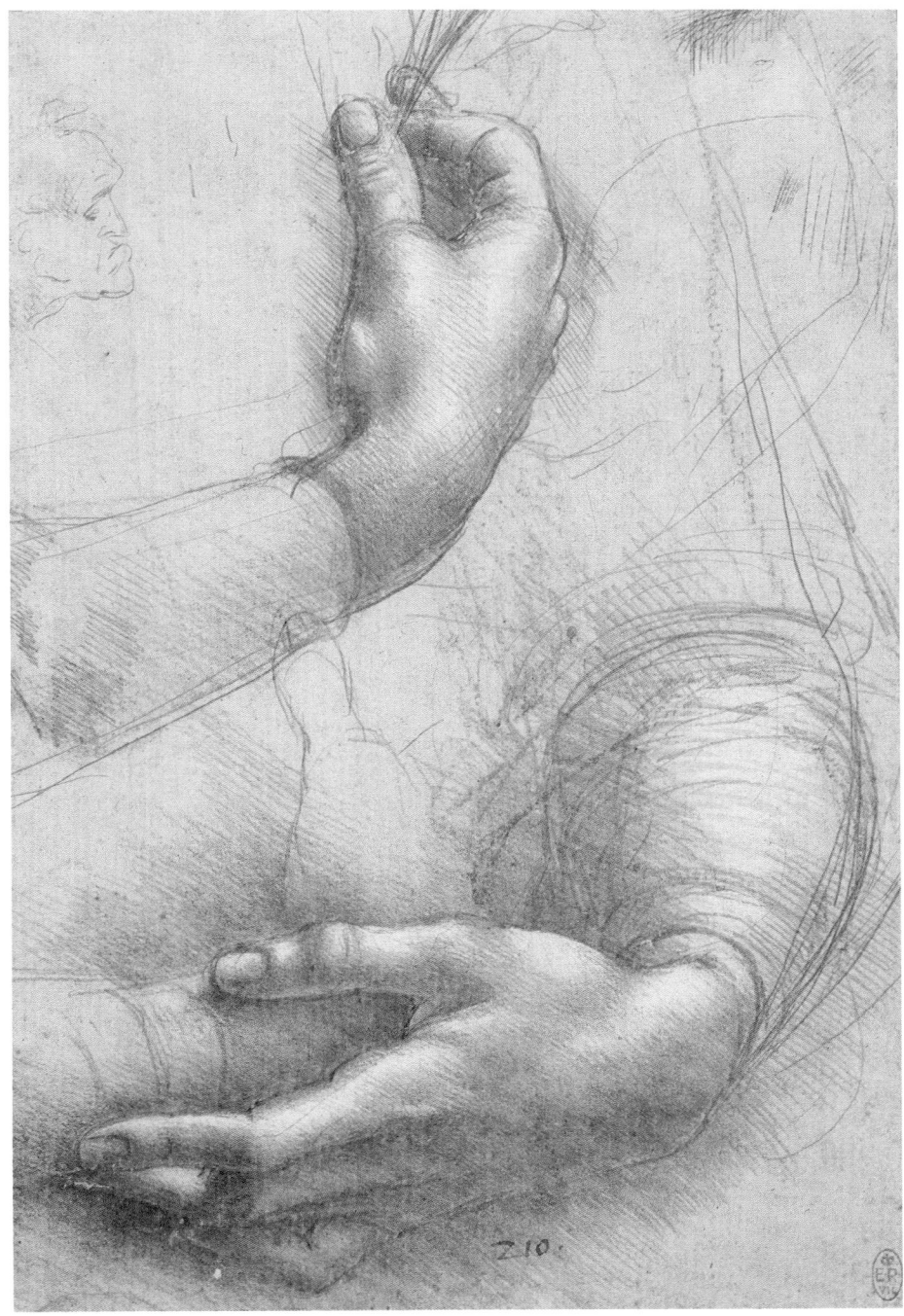

Z10

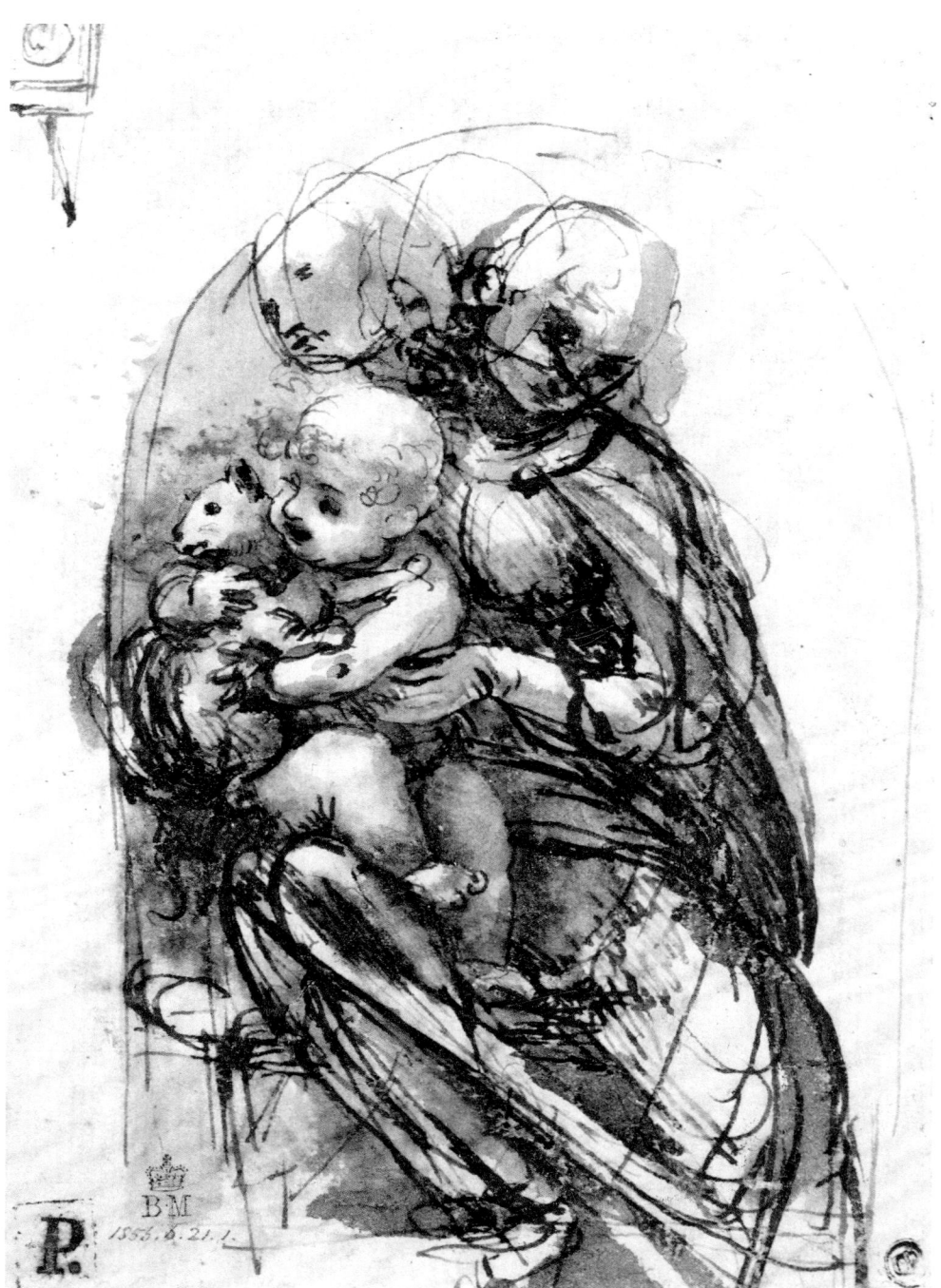

Study for a *Madonna with a Cat*, c.1478–80

Early in April 1476, Leonardo and three other men were denounced to the Office of the Night for the crime of sodomy. The victim (or willing partner) who was the subject of this activity was Jacopo Saltarelli, a 17-year-old model. The Office of the Night acted as a morality police, investigating crimes brought to their notice. Homosexual activity was a serious crime, punishable by public humiliation, corporal punishment, branding and even execution. However, extreme punishments were rarely enacted and there was a degree of latitude (even acceptance) of homosexuality, especially among the intellectual and political elite of Florence. Many Florentine artists were known to be homosexual. Straddling the line between artisan and courtier, rubbing shoulders with barber-surgeons, prostitutes and actors—often flitting between patrons—artists were granted a degree of moral latitude due to their peripatetic circumstances.

Leonardo was apparently arrested and questioned regarding that accusation. On 7 June the group was acquitted without trial, possibly due to political pressure behind the scenes. One of the co-accused was part of the Medici clan. It is casually assumed that Leonardo was supported by the Medici family, but he received no commissions to paint for them. Leonardo designed pageant costumes and theatrical scenery for the court and would have met many leading lights of the Medici circle. However, painting projects of the Medici went to Botticelli, Ghirlandaio and Perugino. In the summer of 1481, a group of skilled Florentine painters was sent to the Vatican by Lorenzo de' Medici

(1449–1492); Leonardo was not among them. For whatever reason, he did not fit in at the Medici court at this time.

Leonardo stayed with Verrocchio until 1477, when he then established a studio of his own; he may have still collaborated with his former master after then. It was an unusually delayed independence for such a talented artist, who had qualified as a master in 1472. Unlike a journeyman, unable to invent new compositions, most artists of Leonardo's ability would have opened their own workshop before the age of twenty-five. It seems Leonardo was aware he was not suited for business, being both a slow painter and poor negotiator, as we shall see later.

On 10 January 1478 Leonardo received his first independent commission. It was an altarpiece showing the vision of St Bernard. Never executed, this would become the first of many failed commissions. Another was designing a tapestry (on the topic of Adam and Eve) for the king of Portugal, which was never delivered. Leonardo was working on small devotional panels of the Madonna and Child—pieces that might be sold to private individuals. Pages of sketches show him testing out ideas for the Maternities; the most original and touching are those involving the infant holding a (sometimes quite unwilling) cat (page 18). These thumbnail compositional sketches—which apparently commence in the 1470s—are significant in that they are the first surviving drawings showing an artist changing designs in single sketches. Their lively spontaneous qualities allow us to inhabit Leonardo's mind as he discovers ideas and checks

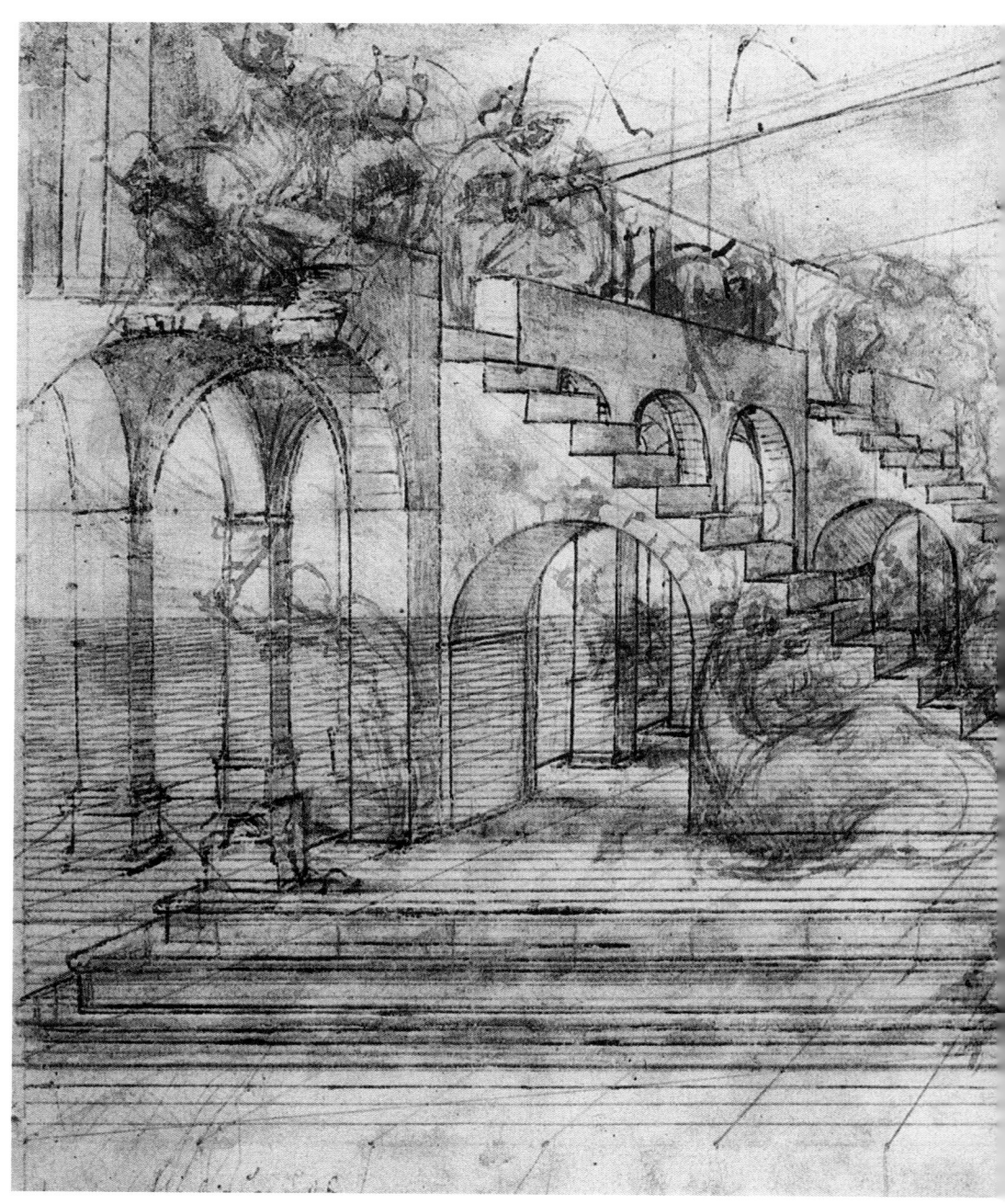

Perspective Study for the Background of the Adoration of the Magi, 1481

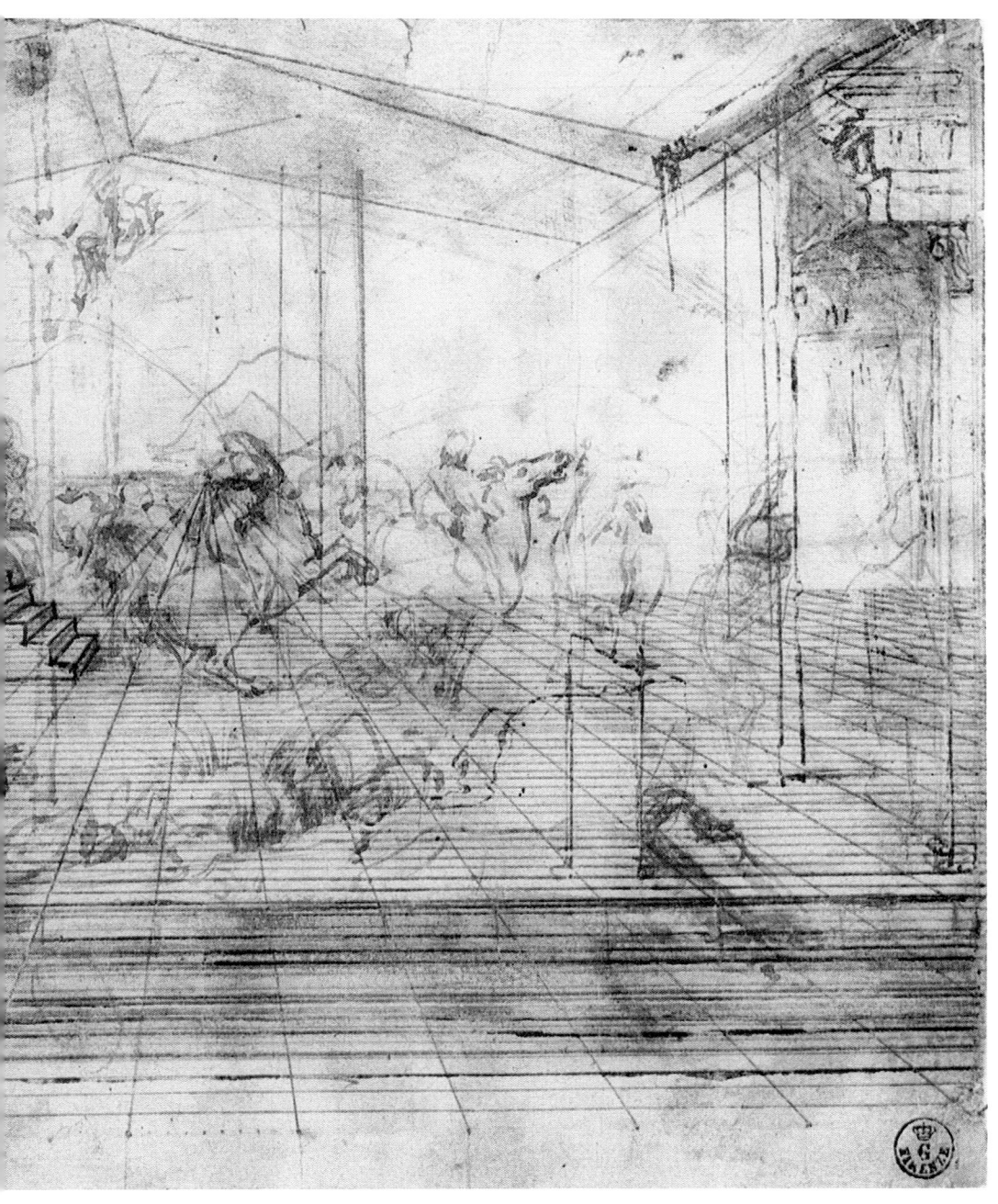

21

alternative solutions. While earlier artists may have worked out ideas in similar ways, these are the oldest surviving drawings of this type, preserved because of their instructional value.

By the time he was contracted to produce a large painting (in March 1481), Leonardo was anxious for work. Not only was he in need of money, he had yet to make his mark as he approached thirty. His days as the golden youth of Verrocchio's studio were over and he had no substantial achievement to his name. Leonardo was never wealthy although later (when income permitted) he kept up to six pupils, assistants and servants at the same time, as well as purchasing fine clothes, books, materials, curiosities and pets. Straitened circumstances explain why Leonardo was willing to accept a new commission on unfavourable terms.

The artist agreed to paint a scene of the Adoration of the Magi for an Augustinian monastery (page 55). He embarked on a series of elaborate studies of remarkable rigour, complexity and inventiveness. It was as if a dam had burst. Numerous studies of figures and animals show Leonardo's unwillingness to rely on second-hand ideas. A perspectival sketch (pages 20/1) bristles with dynamism; vivid incidents animate the deep pictorial space, hinting at a world rich with unlimited events. Terms of the agreement were inconvenient and not remunerative. Leonardo could not afford the pigments necessary and requested the monks pay extra for those. The primary reason for the failure to complete the panel was—as it almost always was with Leonardo—internal not situational. It seems that once Leonardo had solved the problems he set himself, finished objects held no appeal.

Over the winter of 1481/2, with his brilliant *Adoration* unfinished and nothing important to his public credit, new opportunities opened up for the painter. Leonardo relocated to Milan, being either sent by Lorenzo de' Medici or requested by Ludovico Sforza (1452–1508), Duke of Milan (interpretations differ). Milan was the capital of the powerful strategically important region of Lombardy. Larger than Florence, Milan was a growing and rich city with a prosperous arms trade. With the exception of its impressive cathedral, it lacked visual culture. The talented but erratic painter-engineer would become a diplomatic gift from Florence to its ally.

What is striking about the draft letter Leonardo wrote to Ludovico (composed that winter) was that he chose to emphasise his credentials as an engineer, architect and inventor. The draft states Leonardo could make "light and strong bridges, easily portable", drain trenches, destroy fortifications, design cannon and bombardment devices, dig underground tunnels and even construct armoured tanks. Only finally did he add "in painting I can do everything that is possible to do" and was able to design and cast an equestrian statue. Ludovico had announced a wish to honour his father's memory with a horse and rider, to be cast in bronze and larger than any previous. It was a technically ambitious project that caught the imagination of artists; as yet, Ludovico had not approved any specific proposal. Cannily, Leonardo knew that the duke's military needs were more

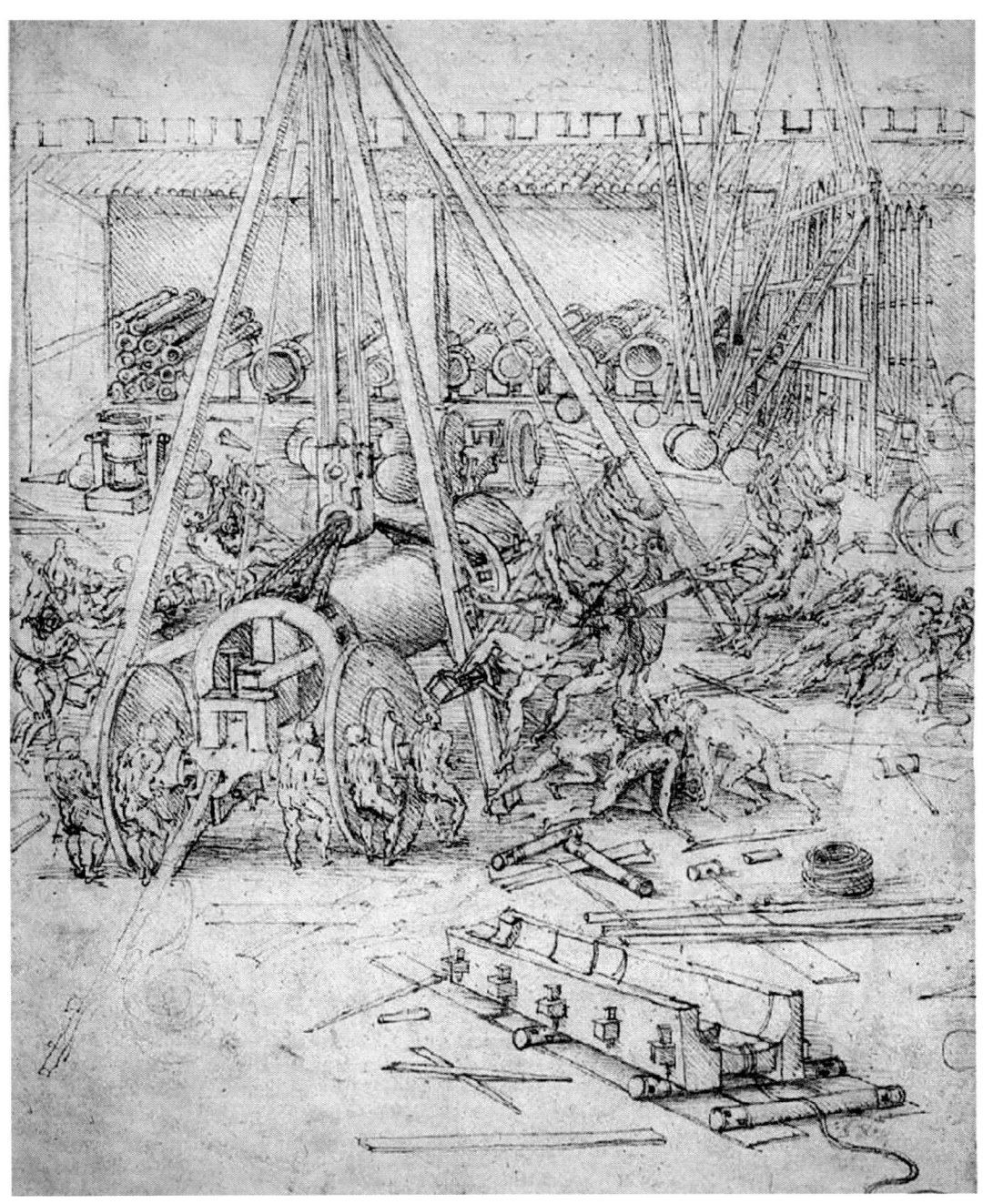

A Scene in an Arsenal, c. 1487

pressing and that proving himself as the duke's engineer-in-chief would make him first in line to design the monument.

By February 1482, Leonardo was in Milan, performing as a musician for Ludovico; he sang and played a silver lyre (a form of violin) which he had designed like a horse's head. Ludovico Sforza was an intelligent and ambitious man, although fickle. He acted as duke regent on behalf of his young nephew from 1476, then later on his own behalf, following the death of his nephew; it was widely supposed Ludovico had him poisoned in 1494 to gain outright power. Ludovico (called "Il Moro", the Moor) reigned for over two decades, no mean feat in an era of domestic scheming and foreign conflict. Leonardo would call Milan home until 1499 and during that period he would be close to Ludovico in a way he never had been to Lorenzo de' Medici.

In Leonardo's sketchbooks we find innumerable designs for cannons, ballistic weapons, siege engines and fortifications as well as estimated missile trajectories. Some are derived from observation. The drawing of a cannon being assembled in a military yard (page 23) derives from what Leonardo had already seen; the extraordinary size of the cannon is a boastful invention. He knew that Italians were concerned because the French had superior armaments. That Leonardo was revolted by cruelty and war seems contradictory for a military engineer, yet if we think of him as wanting to make weapons so powerful that they would end warfare, we can see him attempting to be a man of peace. That said, clearly Leonardo was so fas-

cinated by the challenge of improving and inventing devices, that he could forget the ends to which those weapons would be put. In practice, few of Leonardo's weapons would ever be built.

Modern recreations of these machines have yielded mixed results. Generally, Leonardo correctly intuited principles behind mechanical devices, but the materials and techniques needed did not exist in his time. Most famous of his inventions were flying devices that he called *uccelli* (Italian: birds). Fascinated by birds and bats, Leonardo devised prototypical gliders, helicopters and parachutes. Much later (in early January 1496) he constructed a machine he felt confident enough to test. As we have no record of the outcome of his attempt, we must assume it failed or was not tried. The principles for Leonardo's gliders and parachutes were sound but his machines for powered flight were unfeasible.

In 1483 Leonardo was commissioned to paint an altarpiece for the Confraternity of the Immaculate Conception, Milan. This time not only did Leonardo deliver, he would eventually make two versions of the painting. *The Virgin of the Rocks* depicts the Virgin Mary, the infant Christ, the infant St John the Baptist and archangel Uriel, situated in a cave or rocky cleft (pages 57 and 77). The figures are seen surrounded by a bare rock, allowing Leonardo to indulge his fascination with petrology. He worked in collaboration with the de Predis brothers, a Milanese family of artists and craftsmen. Ambrogio de Predis (c. 1455– c. 1508) is credited with the enchanting profile portrait of a lady (page 25), considered a potential portrait of Beatrice d'Este or

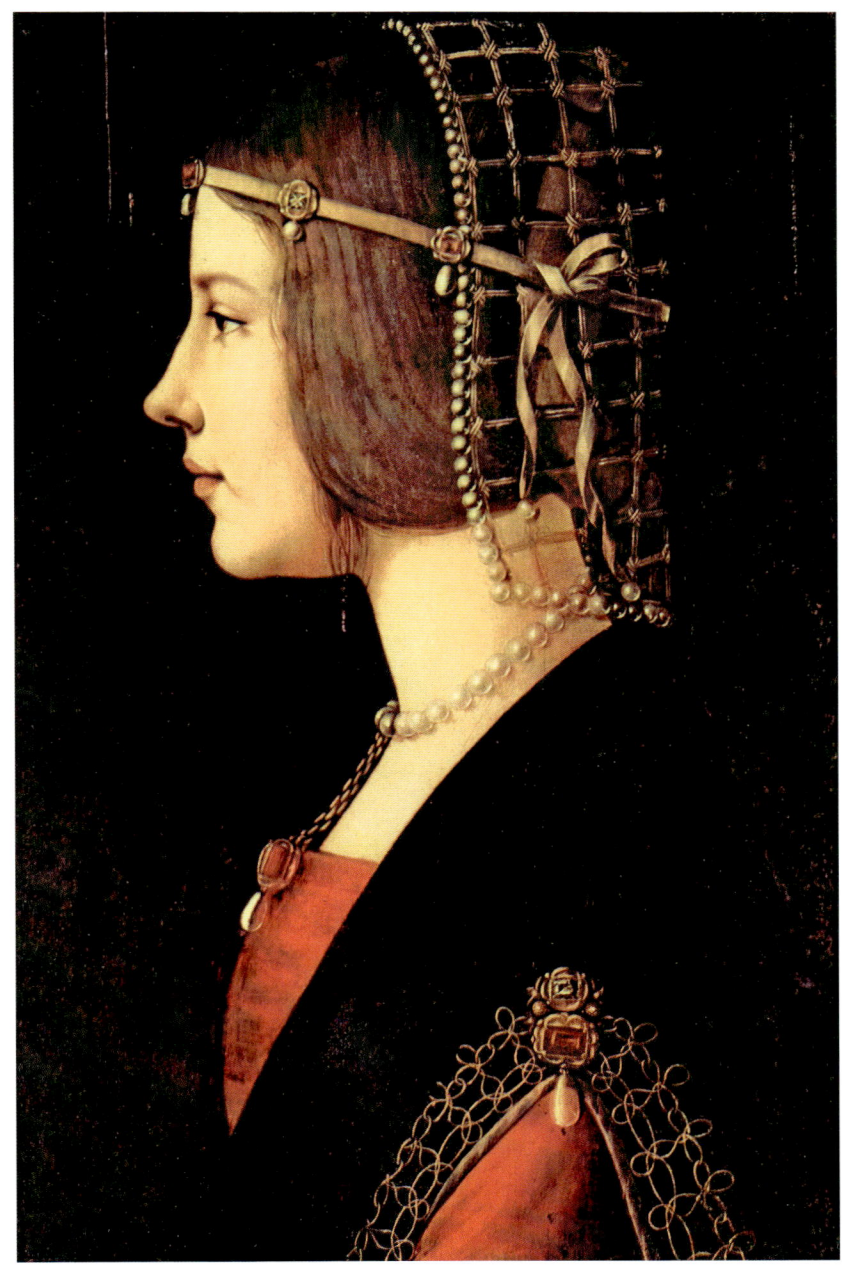

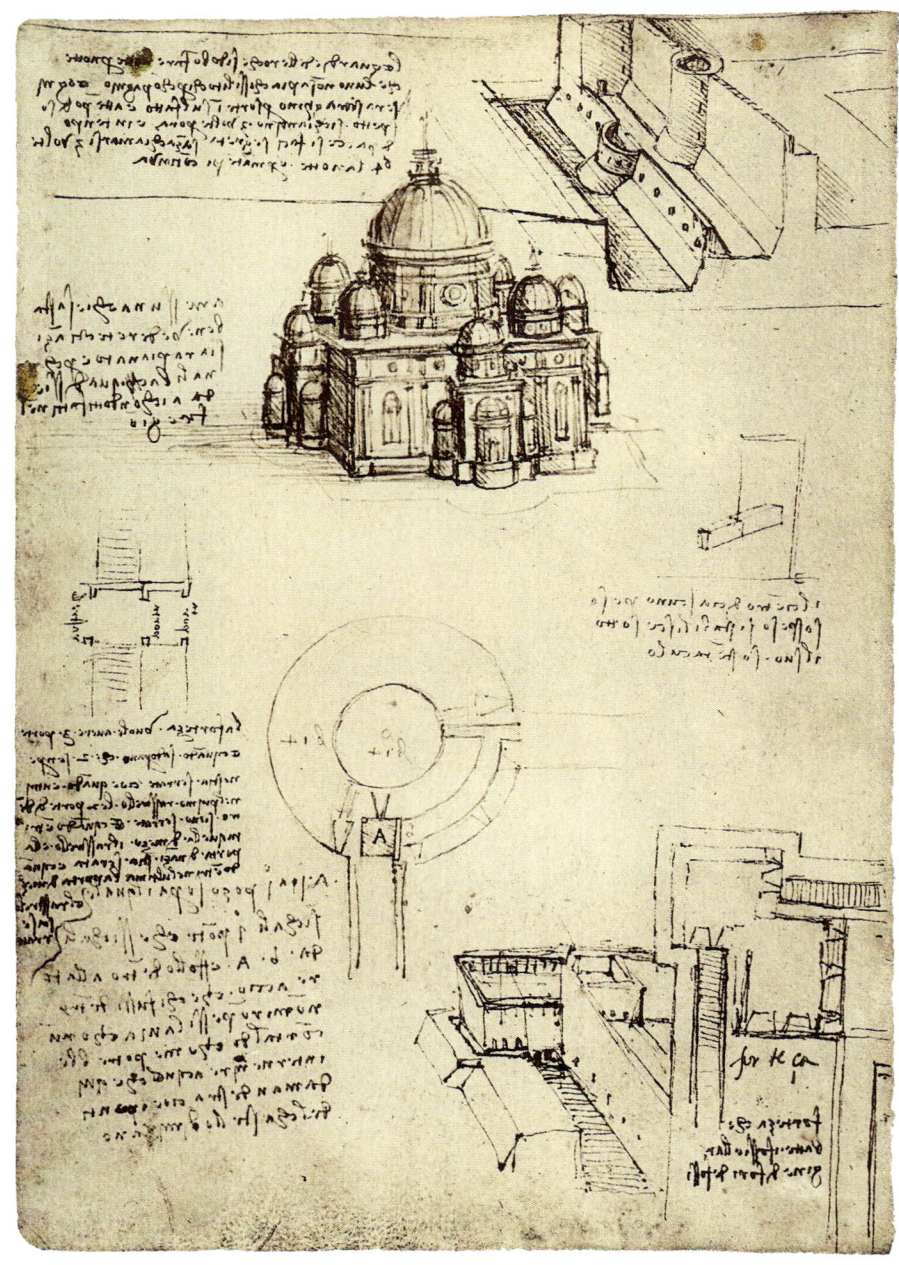

View and Plan of a Square Church with a Central Dome and Four Cupolas. 1488

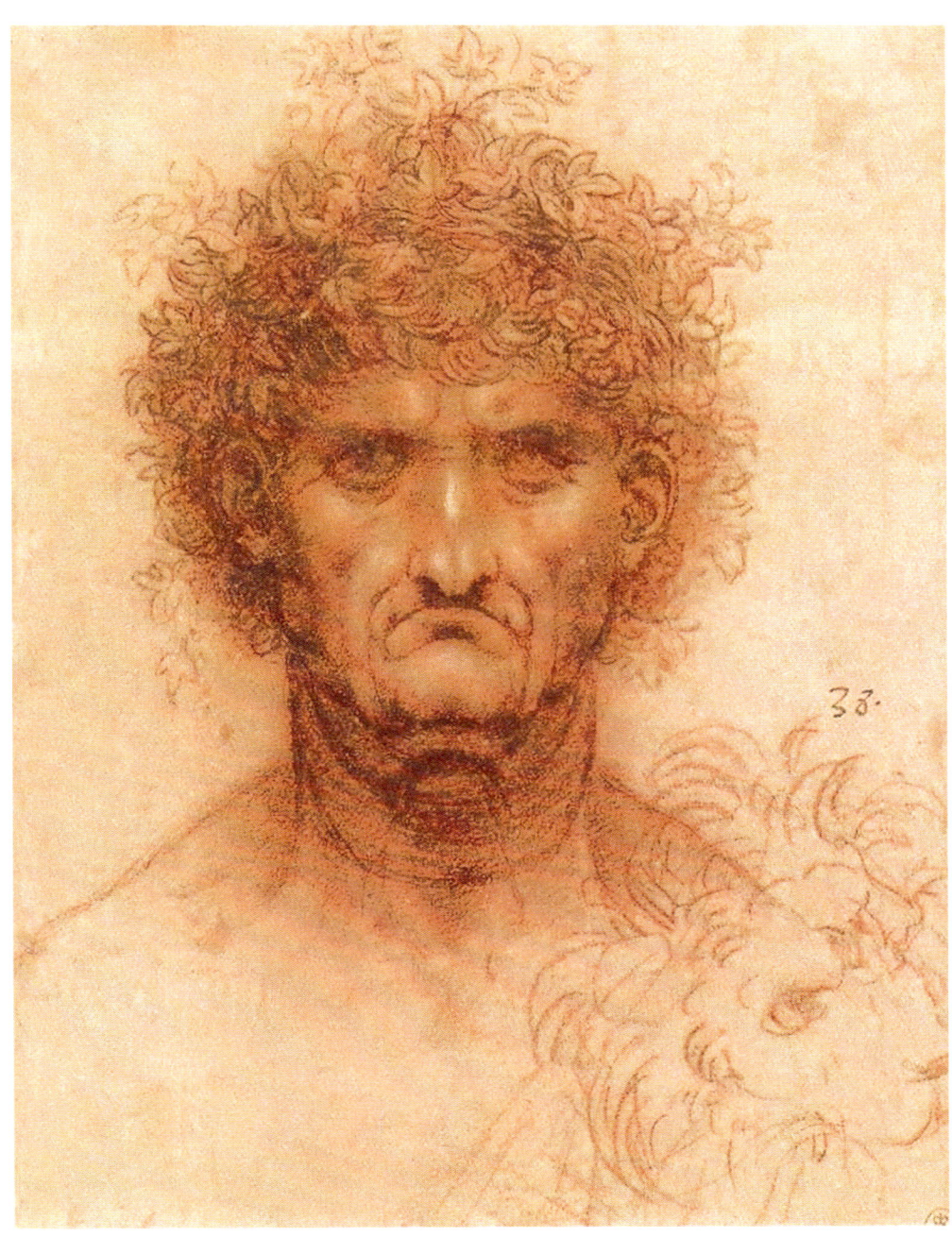

Character Head of an Older Man and Sketch of a Lion's Head, c. 1505–10

Anna Maria Sforza, daughter of Il Moro. Many have wondered if Leonardo contributed in some way to this portrait.

Once again the painter was involved in a wrangle regarding payment, claiming (reasonably) that he had been paid too little and too late for the altarpiece (now in the Louvre). It is unclear why a second version came to be made; perhaps the first version was bought by Il Moro from the confraternity, with the second version being a substitute. The duke was beginning to appreciate Leonardo's painting. In addition to possibly acquiring the first *Virgin of the Rocks*, Ludovico may have commissioned the portrait of a musician (page 59). Definite approval is signalled by commissions to paint the duke's mistresses Cecilia Gallerani (page 65), then later Lucrezia Crivelli (page 75).

Leonardo travelled frequently; in the 1480s, in order to record his many activities, he started keeping notebooks. These varied in size and binding and are now preserved in museums and royal collections in Paris, London, Madrid, Milan and Turin. In them we find notes on many subjects, draft letters, lists of things to do, recipes for varnishes, expense accounts and mathematical problems, all interspersed with drawings. These often chaotic journals are working papers and not diaries. There is (with a few exceptions) little about private feelings, encounters and memories. Despite being wary of retrospectively diagnosing conditions, we should consider the case for Leonardo as having had Attention Deficit Disorder. Considering his propensity for intense activity and concentrated focus—as well being easily distracted and break-

ing off activities for which he was well suited (and well paid)—the pattern of this condition maps on well to Leonardo's known behaviour, for which his notebooks are prime evidence.

The notebooks are written in Leonardo's characteristic right-to-left script, developed to suit his left-handedness. Although it made his private writings difficult to follow (albeit easily read with a mirror), the script was primarily a matter of convenience rather than secrecy. Despite the fact that thousands of pages survive, they form perhaps only about a quarter of the original amount. Leonardo declared that he would write treatises on painting, human anatomy, bird flight, hydrodynamics and other subjects. Disappointed by the quality of woodcut illustrations, he developed a new method of relief printing by transferring drawings to iron plates. This would have been the ideal method of illustrating his treatises had they ever been published.

Over 1487/8, Leonardo was a participant competing to design a dome for the Milan cathedral. His proposal was not selected but it comprised part of his recurrent interest in architectural construction (page 26). He designed churches, villas, streets and town centres, as well as fortifications for patrons. None of these designs were built in his day but plans for a royal palace in France influenced a later generation of French royal architects. In 1489, after making countless drawings and small *modelli* in clay and wax, the draft for the Sforza horse was complete. Leonardo received approval to make a full-size model. The giant *modello* (of clay over an armature of wood and iron) was con-

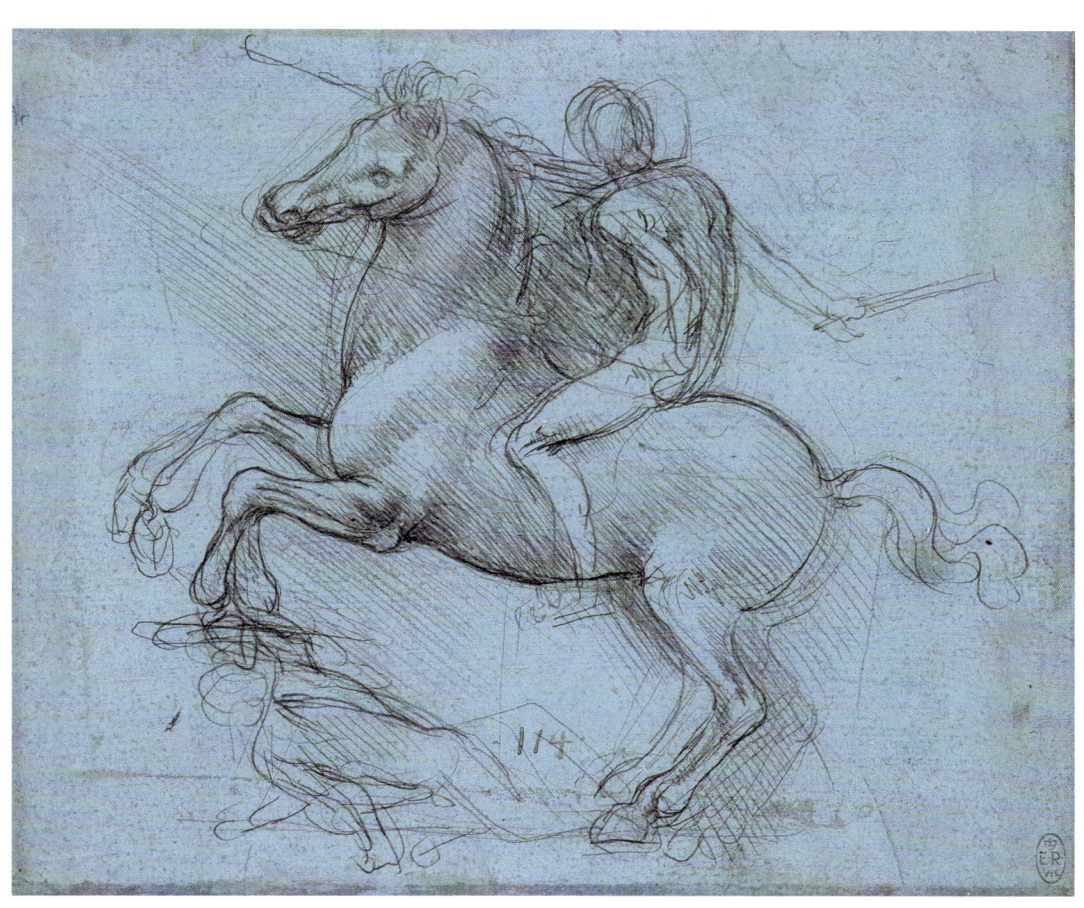

Study for the Sforza Monument, c. 1488

structed during 1492/3. Ultimately, war intervened and the monument was not realised.

In the summer of 1490, a new person entered Leonardo's life—Gian Giacomo Caprotti da Oreno (1480–1524). Leonardo called him "Salaì" (little devil). The angelic appearance of this young companion-assistant, with his pretty face and dark ringlets, belied a mischievous disruptive influence. Forever stealing and misbehaving, Salaì caused no end of trouble for master and apprentices, as the notebooks attest. "Thief, liar, obstinate, greedy", declared Leonardo. He kept him on as a model and source of amusement, perhaps as a lover. He spent extravagantly on the youth's clothing. In time, Salaì would become a faithful companion and an indifferent painter.

On a pocketbook page we find an oddly distracted entry. "On the 16th day of July. Caterina came on the 16th day of July 1493." Biographers have extensively debated whether or not this woman was Leonardo's mother or a servant. Does that peculiar slip of Leonardo's concentration (the double dating of the event) betoken suppressed strong emotion? There is no definite inference to be drawn from this slip nor from a dry accounting of her modest funeral expenses in 1494 or 1495. Leonardo noted the death date of his father but not of his mother—at least, not in the pages we have.

For the dining room of a Milan monastery, Il Moro commissioned from Leonardo an image of Christ's Last Supper with his Disciples—a traditional subject for such settings. The resultant *Last Supper* (c. 1495–7) (page 81) would become considered Leonardo's supreme achievement, with its fame spread through painted and engraved copies. As Verrocchio's workshop did not paint frescoes, Leonardo was never instructed in that technique. His unconventional tempera-oil mix imparted unprecedented naturalism but it would prove impermanent; the mural would be a ruin in Leonardo's lifetime.

Leonardo met mathematician-friar Luca Pacioli (c. 1455–1517) when the latter arrived to serve the Milan court in 1496. They would become friends and travelling companions. Pacioli introduced Leonardo to Euclid's geometry, which became a persistent subject of study in coming decades. Leonardo provided designs for woodcut illustrations of mathematical objects in Pacioli's book *Divina Proportione* (1498). At this time the painter attempted to learn Latin in order to gain access to knowledge in books of science and philosophy. Despite taking pride in being a "disciple of experience", Leonardo was acutely aware of his lack of familiarity with topics discussed by the intellectuals at court.

In August 1499 the army of French King Louis XII entered the Duchy of Milan. Led by Marshal Trivulzio, the army committed a series of massacres as it made rapid progress towards Milan city. After initial resistance, the city surrendered and Il Moro fled. It seems Leonardo worked for the French briefly, then departed Milan in early 1500. Readers will be permitted for getting confused about Leonardo's exact location over the next years. From 1500 to 1506 the artist spent most of his time in Florence, but with long periods elsewhere; between 1506 and 1513 he was mostly in Milan.

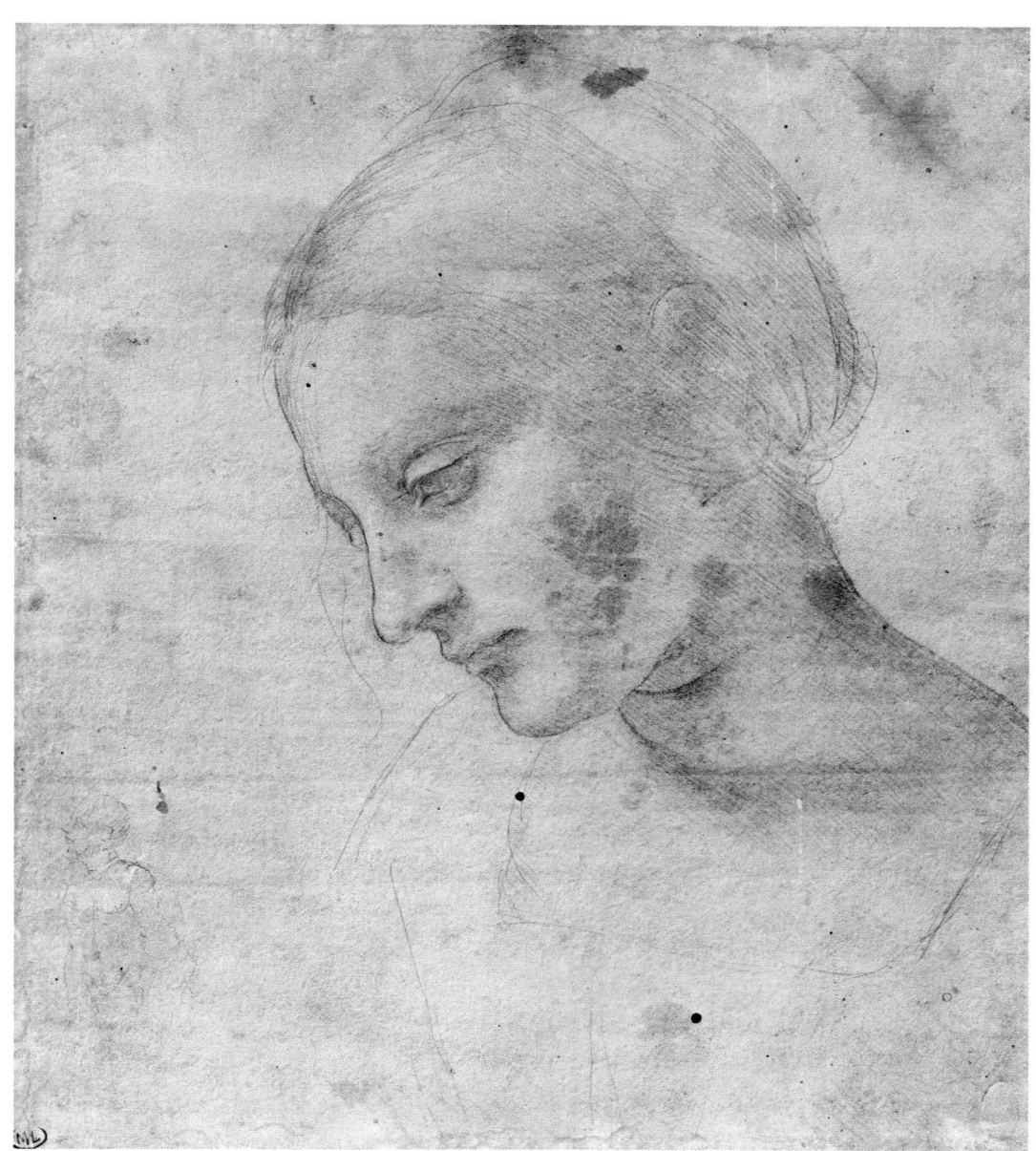

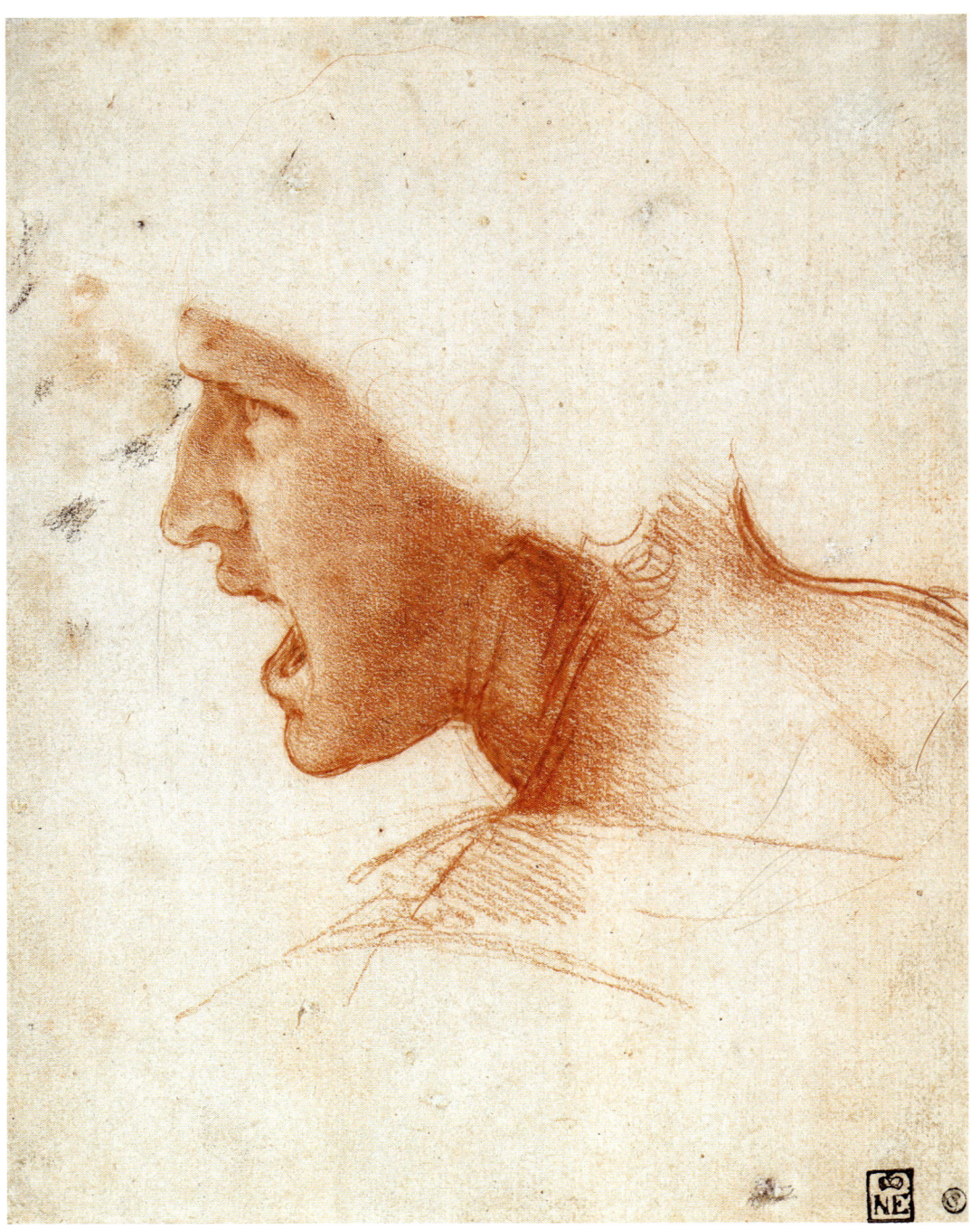

Head of a Man Shouting in Profile, 1504/5

Without a patron, Leonardo travelled first to Mantua. Soon after, he was in Venice with Pacioli. In spring 1500, in a Venetian canal, Leonardo tested an elaborate prototype diving suit, complete with weights and buoyancy devices. The aim was to see if it would be possible for divers to sink moored ships by drilling holes from beneath. Although the equipment proved satisfactory, Leonardo declined to perfect or share his plans because he considered drowning mariners who were unaware of their peril to be a dishonourable action.

Leonardo's ideas on defining physical forms through shading rather than line (called *sfumato*) impressed Venetian artists. We know frustratingly little of whom Leonardo met in Venice and what (aside from some notebooks) he had with him to show others, apart from an unfinished portrait of Isabella d'Este. Particularly receptive to Leonardo's aesthetic ideas was the young Giorgione (1477–1510), who made delicate shading and uniformly dark backgrounds key parts of his style. In turn, Giorgione's technique was absorbed by Titian and Tintoretto and came to characterise Venetian Renaissance art.

Cesare Borgia (1475–1507), variously a cardinal, mercenary and warlord, acted as head general of the Papal States, doing the will of his father Pope Alexander VI (r. 1492–1503). Effective, brutal and highly feared, Cesare required engineers and armourers. In the summer of 1502 the gentle and peace-loving artist-scientist joined Cesare's entourage, which included Machiavelli. Cesare was supported by French King Louis XII, so once again Leonardo was in the orbit of the French court,

a fact that would play a part in the artist's last years.

Leonardo was sent to Romagna to survey the topography; a handsome detailed map of Imola resulted from his patient measurement of the city. Shortly after (in the service of Florence, then warily allied to Cesare) Leonardo's advice was taken on depriving Pisa of its lifeline by diverting its river— a plan that never reached fruition. About this period, an observer noted that, "Two of his assistants make copies, and he from time to time adds some touches to them. He devotes much of his time to geometry and has no fondness at all for the paintbrush".

During Leonardo's absence from Florence, the audacious statues of Michelangelo (1475–1564) had won sculptor fame. (Previously, Leonardo's main rival had been Botticelli, about whose painting Leonardo wrote disparagingly.) In 1503 Florentine officials decided to have Michelangelo and Leonardo, both sons of Florence and the greatest living Italian artists, contribute murals to the great hall of the Palazzo Vecchio. Michelangelo chose the Battle of Cascina as his subject; Leonardo elected to paint the Battle of Anghiari, showing victory of the Florentines over the Milanese in 1440 (page 89). Preparatory drawings of warriors (page 32) demonstrate his mastery in depicting fear and anger, extending an engagement with physiological signals, previously explored for *The Last Supper* (page 81). Leonardo designed a composition and painted most of the central motif before his experimental technique (or the materials he had bought) failed. The picture would go uncompleted.

At this time Leonardo (as well as painting religious pictures) commenced the portrait of a silk merchant's wife, the *Mona Lisa* (page 87). In 1507 Francesco Melzi (1491–1570), a member of the minor Milanese nobility, joined Leonardo's service. He was a handsome youth, courtly, cultured and with some artistic training. He was the high-born discreet alter ego to the reckless disruptive Salaì. Melzi would become his master's trusted companion, skilled assistant and dedicated secretary.

It was Melzi's diligence that led (indirectly) to so many of Leonardo's drawings entering the British Royal Collection at Windsor Castle. Melzi preserved Leonardo's drawings, some of which were purchased after his death by sculptor Pompeo Leoni. These albums were acquired by Lord Arundel, who took them from Italy to England. It was Arundel, a monarchist, who probably gave or sold the drawings to the newly restored King of England Charles II (r. 1660–85).

In autumn 1513 Leonardo was summoned to Rome to serve the latest generation of Medici, acting as Florentine artist-emissary to the Vatican, on behalf of Duke Giuliano de' Medici. Rome had a smaller population than Milan and was only just shaking off its reputation as an artistic backwater. Leonardo was given rooms in the Belvedere Courtyard in the Vatican Palace. Rather than being in direct competition with Michelangelo and Raphael (1483–1520)—then both in Rome—it seems Leonardo had practically given up art. Instead, he spent time on experiments and anatomy. The newly appointed Pope Leo X commissioned a painting but grew frustrated when he perceived Leonardo's dilatoriness. By then the artist's reputation for lateness and failure to deliver deterred even sympathetic patrons. The pope would receive nothing from Leonardo.

We see the artist in Rome at a low ebb. He had no appetite for painting; his studies in natural science were slow and impeded by the unco-operative and malicious; his notes and drawings had become chaotically profuse, preventing compilation of the planned treatises. He was haunted by the idea he had achieved nothing. Chalk drawings of deluges show cataclysmic destruction; they seem reflections of Leonardo's own despair. The death of Giuliano in March 1516 meant that Leonardo lost one of his last reasons to be in Rome.

François I (1494–1547, r. 1515–1547), newly crowned French king, had been a long-time admirer of Leonardo. He appointed him court artist that year ("premier painter, engineer and architect to the king"), inviting him to France. In autumn 1516 Leonardo and his retinue (for one last time) packed up his notebooks, paintings and other possessions. Having travelled over the Alps, the group arrived at Cloux, near Amboise, on the banks of the River Loire, where Leonardo would stay at a fortified manor house adjacent to the royal castle. The king would often visit Leonardo and converse with him. (In which language we do not know.) Provided with a home, servant and stipend, Leonardo resided with Melzi and Salaì, without obligation, more an honoured guest than courtier. With Melzi's assistance, Leonardo attempted to turn his notes into a finished manuscript. He started no new paintings but worked infrequently on the *Virgin*

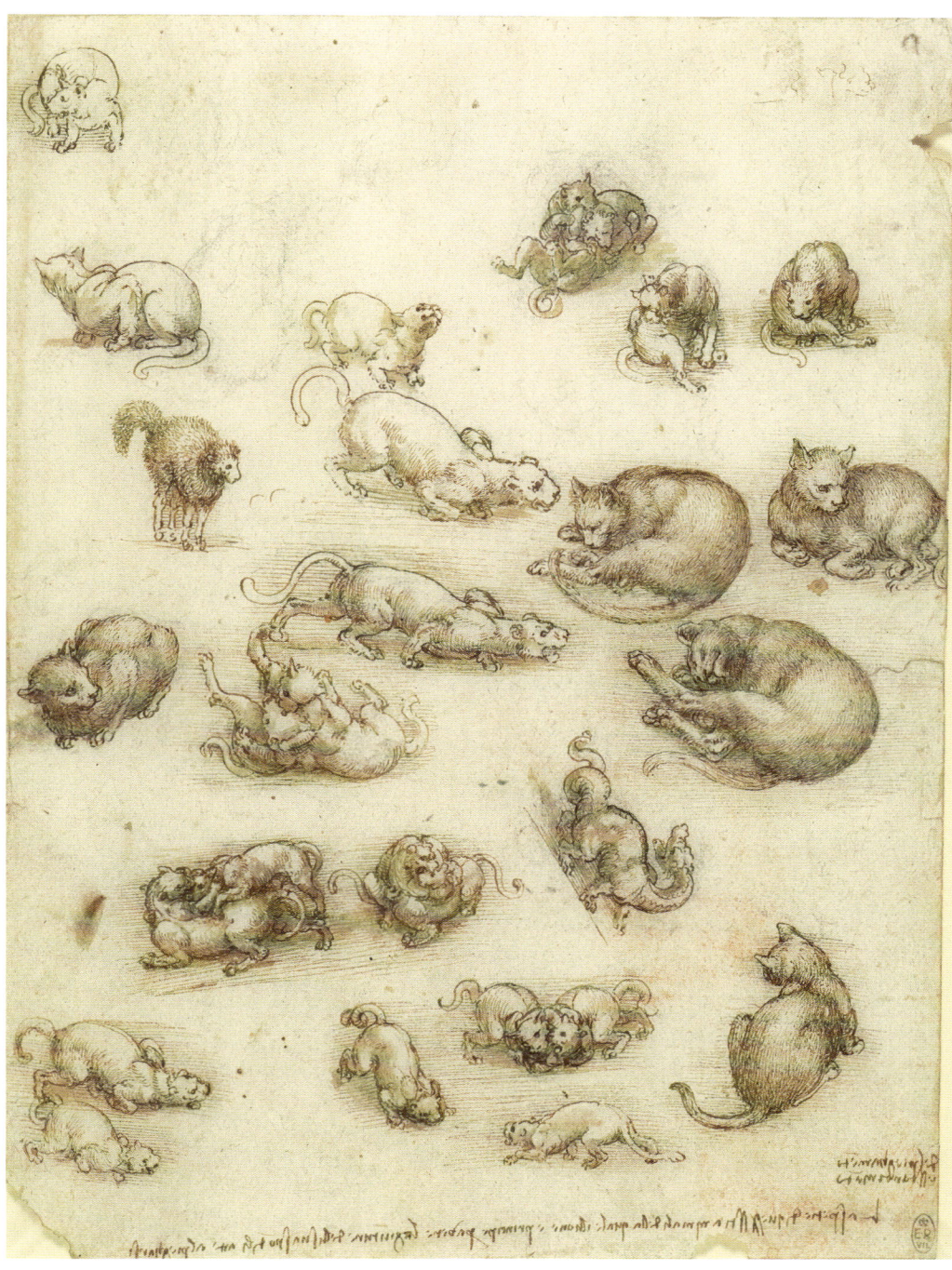

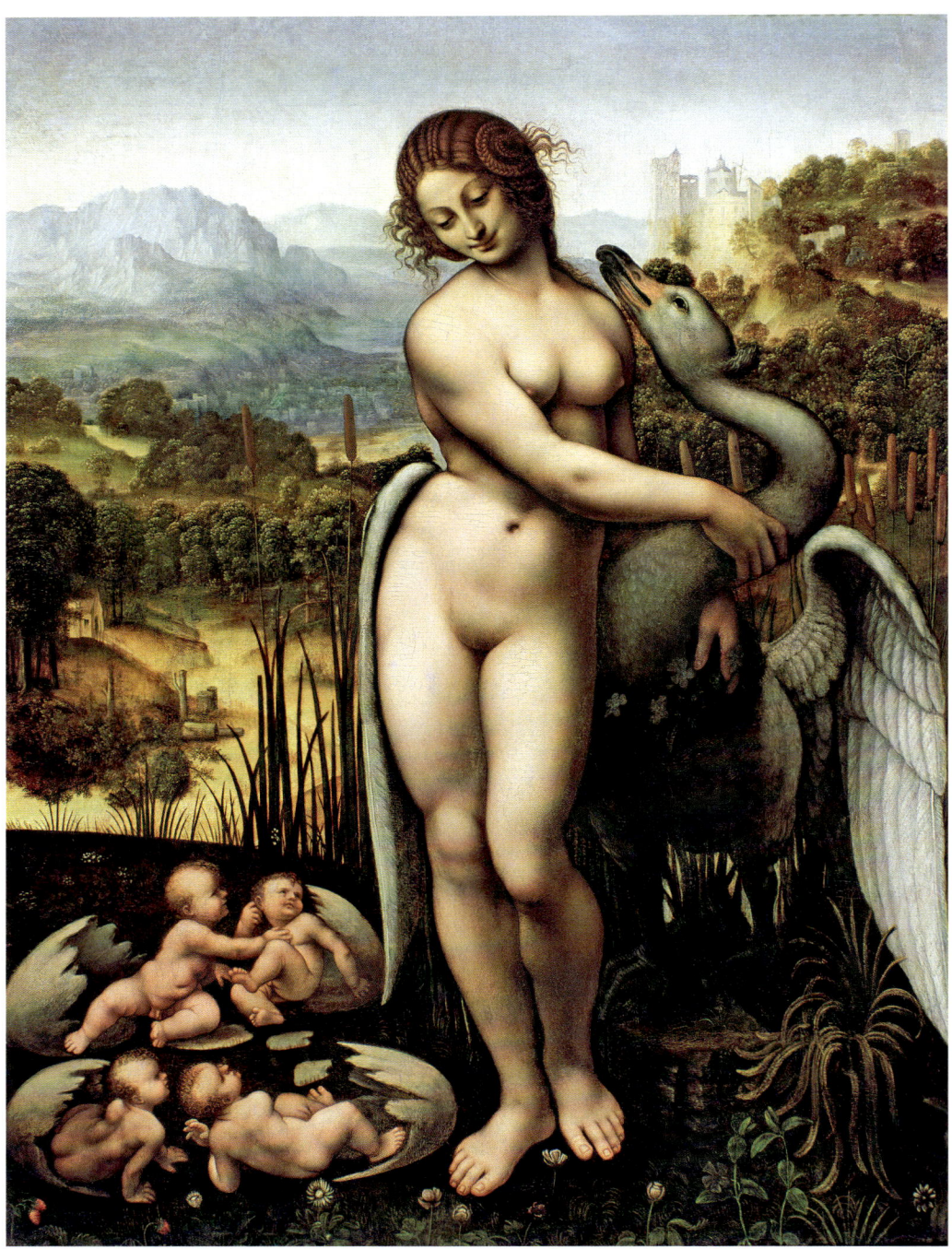

Follower of Leonardo, *Leda and the Swan*, c. 1505–1515

and *St Anne* (page 92) and *St John the Baptist* (page 104).

After his death, Leonardo's few paintings were lost or inaccessible to artists; his two great murals were ruined. Through imitations and copies Leonardo's painting lived on, however inadequately. One such is *Leda*. Although, the original was probably destroyed as morally offensive after Leonardo's death, his idea is fairly represented by at least two extant versions, of which one is illustrated (page 36). In it, Leda presents offspring following her impregnation by Jupiter, disguised as a swan. Leonardo supervised many studio variants, which sometimes diverge radically from each other.

Leonardo wrote his last will and testament on 23 April 1519 with his death recorded on 2 May 1519. Giorgio Vasari (1511–1574) reports Leonardo died in the arms of the King François I. Doubt has been cast on the accuracy of this, but it is clear the king admired the artist tremendously, considering him supremely wise. Leonardo's body was interred locally. Paintings in his collection were sold (or given) to the king by Salaì. Leonardo's executor was Melzi, who inherited his manuscripts and compiled Leonardo's *Treatise on Painting* (completed by 1542, published in 1651). The artist, characteristically, had never finished it himself. A month after Leonardo's death, Melzi wrote touchingly to Leonardo's half-brothers, "He showed to me day by day the warmest love and devotion. It is a hurt to anyone to lose such a man, for nature cannot again produce his like."

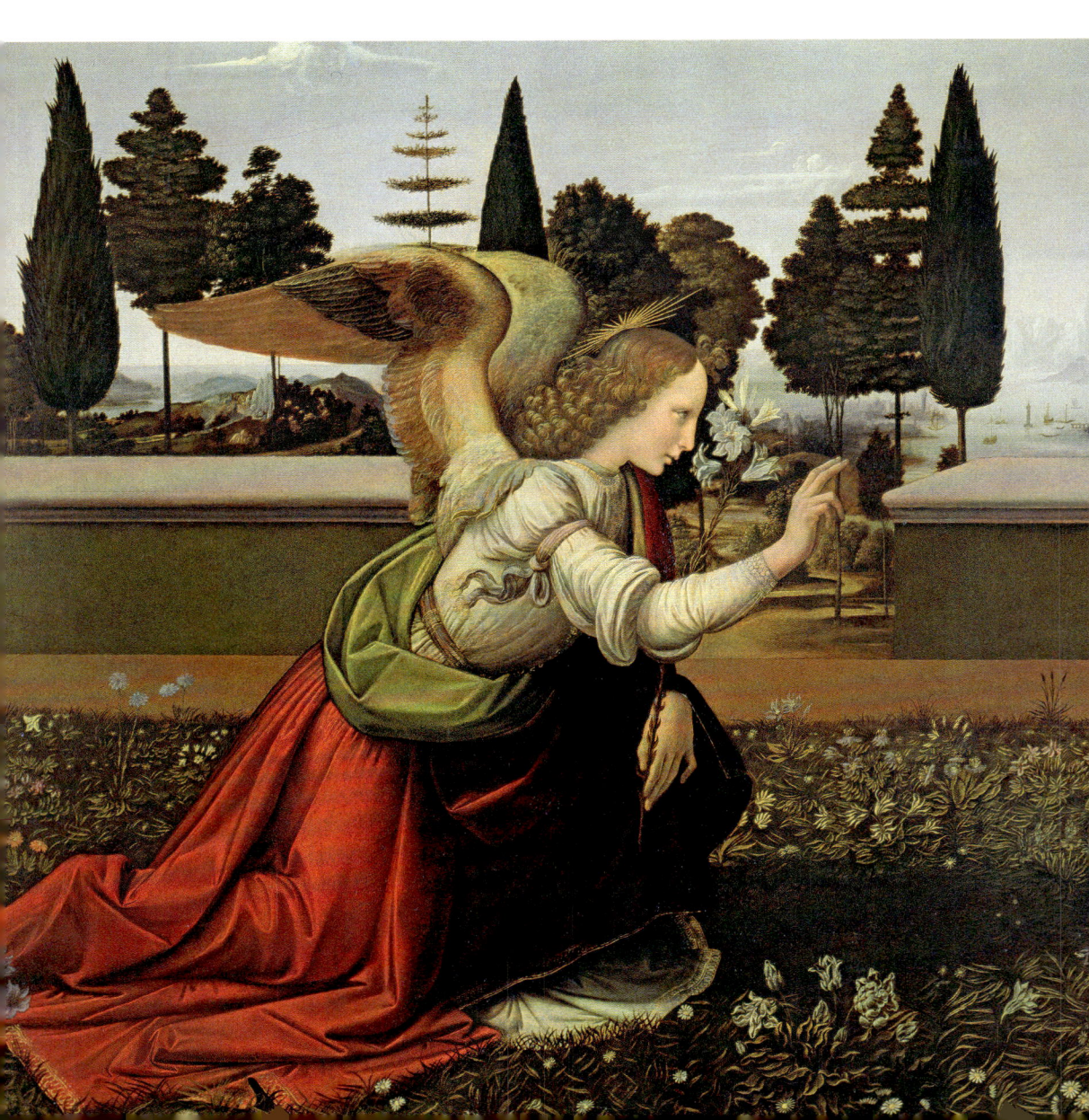

WORKS

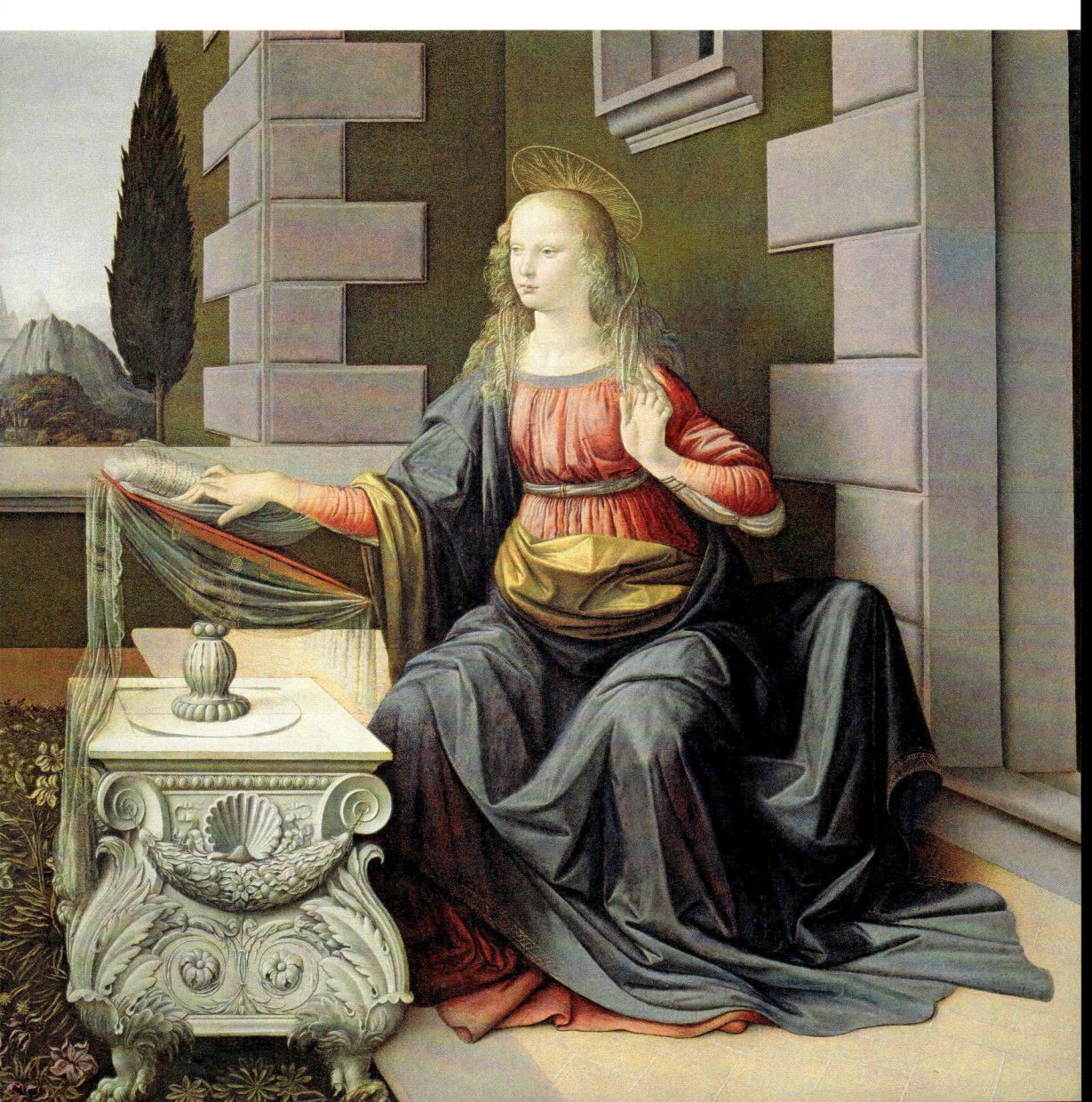

Tobias and the Angel, (c. 1470–2?)

Andrea del Verrocchio, Leonardo da Vinci and assistants
Tempera on poplar
83.6 × 66 cm
The National Gallery, London

In Jewish legend, Tobias was sent by his blinded father Tobit to retrieve some money deposited with a relative in another town. Tobit's prayers for succour were answered by God, who sent archangel Raphael (in human form) to accompany Tobias, who was oblivious to the true nature of his companion. Tobias is told by the archangel that a fish he has caught can be prepared to cure blindness. Thus Tobias is subsequently able to heal Tobit of his condition.

Verrocchio shows Tobias accompanied by Raphael and a dog, as he carries the fish and money back home. Raphael has his gaze fixed upon the fish, which is coincidentally what most recent viewers have paid most attention to. For some years, this painting has been judged the earliest surviving painting towards which Leonardo contributed. Verrocchio was a specialist in sculpture and metalwork; as a painter he was reliable, serious, workmanlike. Almost everything in this picture is consonant with Verrocchio's style: the flat quality of the graceful figures, a perfunctory landscape, sparing detail, crisply legible drapery. (Botticelli is Verrocchio's heir in those respects.) However, the fish is startlingly realistic, with glittering highlights upon the eye and scales. The curving body feels weighty, with its anatomy taken from direct observation. Could this be a work by pupil Leonardo, on the verge of turning twenty years old? Art historians also comment on the liveliness of some of Tobias's curls and the dog's fur, suggesting Leonardo's involvement there. Why might this painting precede *The Baptism of Christ* (page 43)? Verrocchio worked entirely in tempera, although he allowed pupils to adopt the new medium of oil paint. Leonardo would have first been taught tempera painting before training (with whom we do not know) in oils. As this painting is entirely in tempera and we have no other panel paintings by Leonardo solely in tempera (a medium Leonardo soon discarded as inflexible and incapable of the subtlety he required), it is a logical deduction that this painting came before all his others. Another passage potentially painted by Leonardo is the intricate foreshortened carpet in the *Madonna of Piazza*, made in Verrocchio's studio in the 1470s to 1480s.

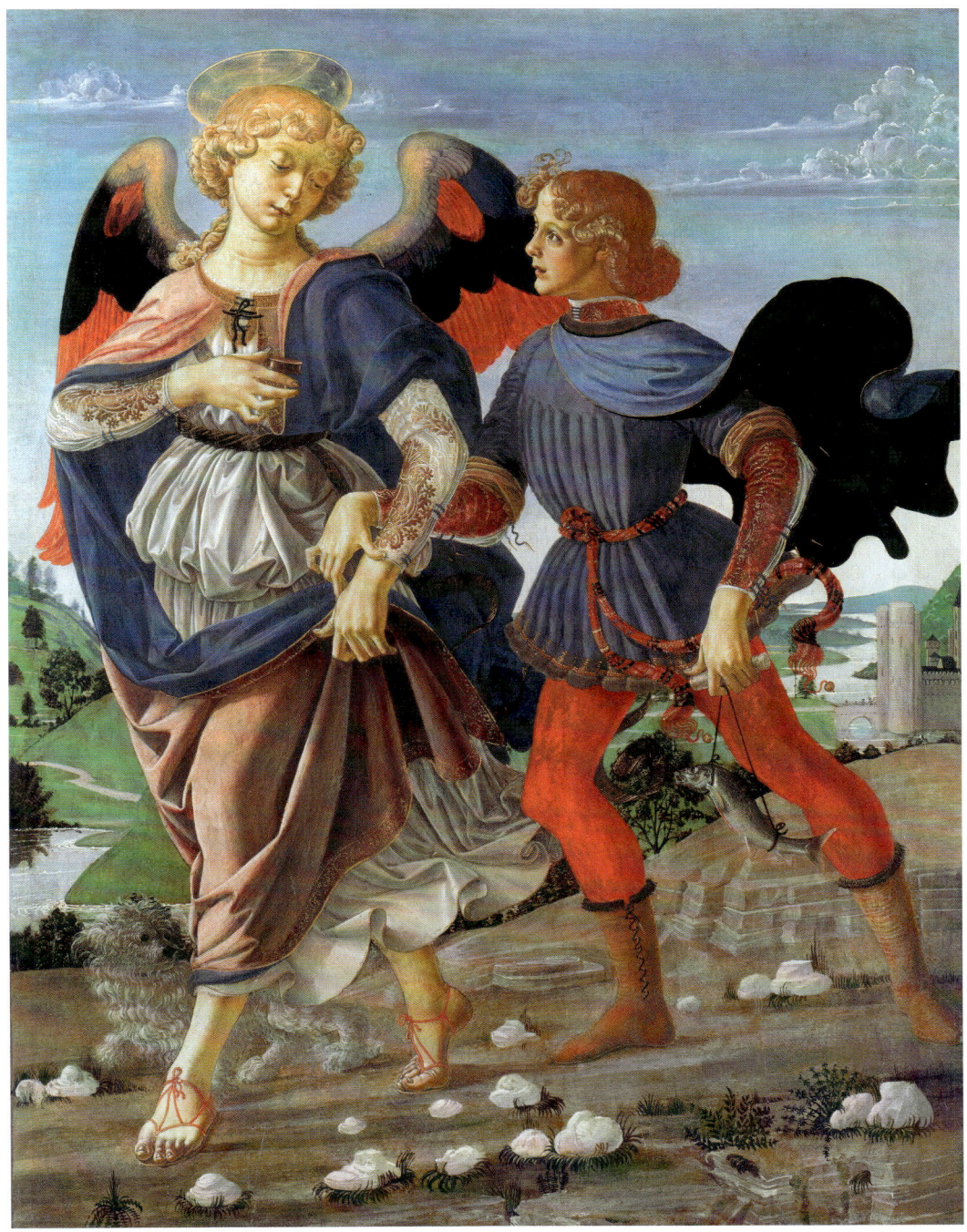

The Baptism of Christ, (c. 1470–2 and c. 1475)

Andrea del Verrocchio, Leonardo da Vinci and assistants
Tempera and oil on poplar
177 × 151 cm
Galleria degli Uffizi, Florence

"[Leonardo] was placed, then, as has been said, in his boyhood, at the instance of Ser Piero, to learn art with Andrea del Verrocchio, who was making a panel-picture of St John baptising Christ, when Leonardo painted an angel who was holding some garments; and although he was but a lad, Leonardo executed it in such a manner that his angel was much better than the figures of Andrea; which was the reason that Andrea would never again touch colour, in disdain that a child should know more than he."

So begins the artistic career of Leonardo, according to Vasari. As is usually the case, Vasari is both correct and fanciful. The painting he describes survives. Its leftmost angel does match Leonardo's early style. Verrocchio did not give up painting, although he was no doubt delighted to entrust painted commissions to his talented young pupil; the master was never an enthusiastic painter. Leonardo famously declared, "It is a poor disciple who does not excel his master." Vasari's implication that Leonardo painted part of the *Baptism* at the beginning of his apprenticeship is false; the young Leonardo would have had years of menial work, drawing practice and painting exercises before he was given his angel to paint. This is the earliest documented painting worked on by Leonardo but *Tobias and the Angel* (page 41) may date earlier. In recent years, art historians have been scouring the output of Verrocchio's studio (as well as anonymous Florentine paintings from the late 1460s and 1470s) for overlooked Leonardos.

The majority of the painting is in tempera but Leonardo's angel is painted in oils, which contributes to its glowing delicacy. Leonardo is also credited with the distant landscape and perhaps parts of the Christ figure. The softness of the facial modelling, naturalness of the drapery and the glimmering highlights on the hair of the angel amply demonstrate his formidable concentration and powers of observation, which would gain his art so many admirers.

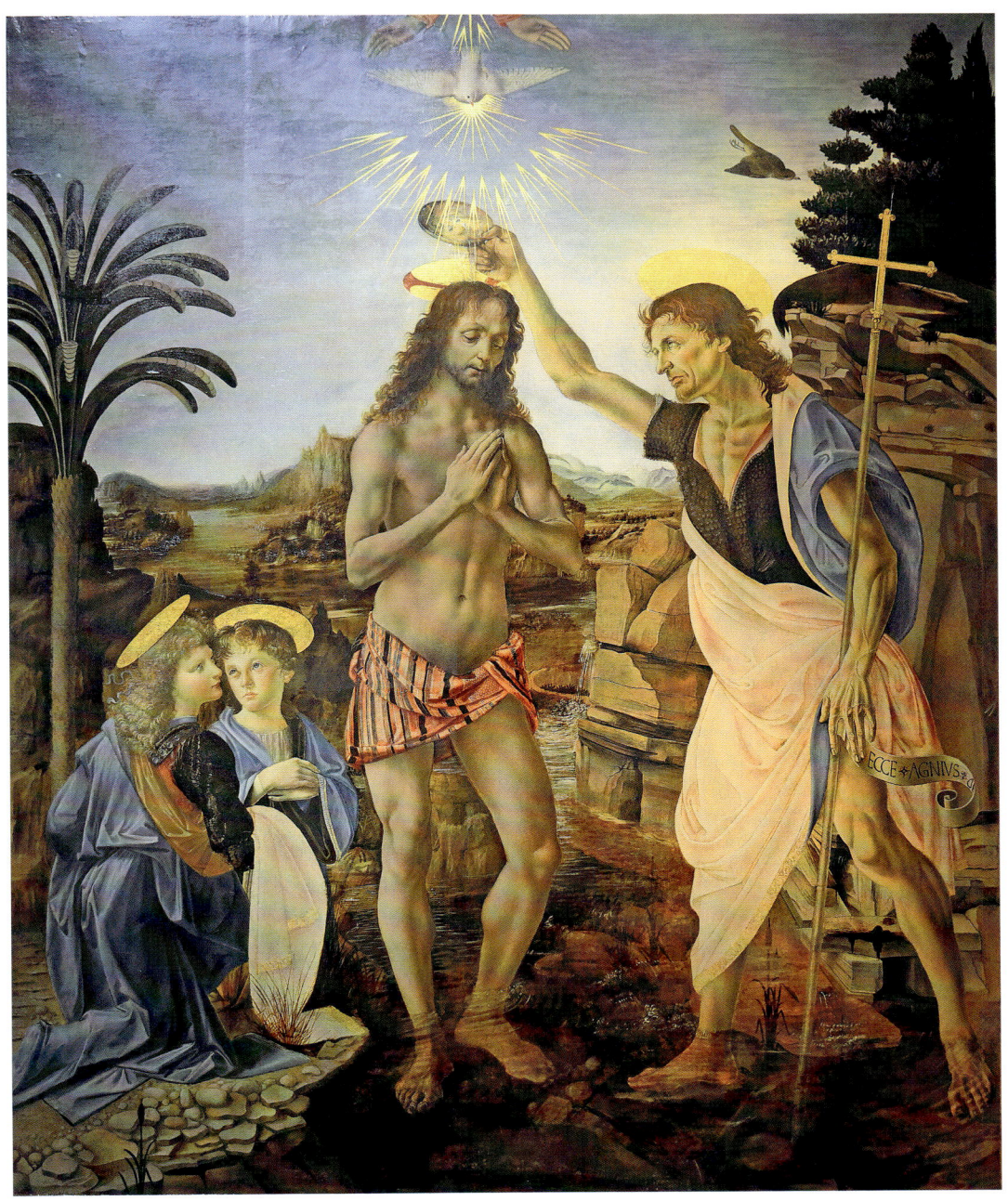

Bust of a Warrior (c. 1472)

Metalpoint with white on prepared cream paper
28.7 × 21.1 cm
The British Museum, London

Writers describe this drawing by the youthful Leonardo (made while he was a pupil) as a copy of a bust of Persian King Darius by Verrocchio. Versions of this warrior in an elaborate helmet appear in many sculptures made in Verrocchio's studio over the 1470s. They show the veneration accorded to ancient sculpture (especially bas reliefs) during the Italian Renaissance. This pugnacious warrior, generally seen as a profile, would become a recurring character in Leonardo's private drawings, often posed facing an angelic teenaged boy.

Although he practised sculpture through much of his career, Leonardo considered painting the highest art. He participated in the common practice of the *paragone* (the debate about the superiority and inferiority of different art forms). Here is his disparagement of sculptors: "The painter has ten considerations with which he is concerned in finishing his works, namely light, shade, colour, body, shape, position, distance, nearness, motion and rest; the sculptor has only to consider body, shape, position, motion and rest. With light and shade he does not concern himself, because nature produces them for his sculpture. Of colour there is none. With distance and closeness he only concerns himself in part, in that he only uses linear perspective [in reliefs] but not the perspective of colour which varies in hue and distinctness of outline with different distances from the eye. Therefore sculpture has fewer considerations and consequently is less demanding of talent than painting." Verrocchio trained Leonardo in sculpture as well as painting and the latter clearly aspired to match his master in sculpture. Given the dearth of verifiably autograph Leonardo sculptures, what his achievements actually were is now impossible for us to assess. We should not neglect consideration of Leonardo's later rivalry with Michelangelo, an acknowledged genius in the field of carved sculpture, when we recall his fluctuating attitudes towards the medium. Leonardo wanted to be the greatest sculptor in the world whilst also dismissing the art form as inferior.

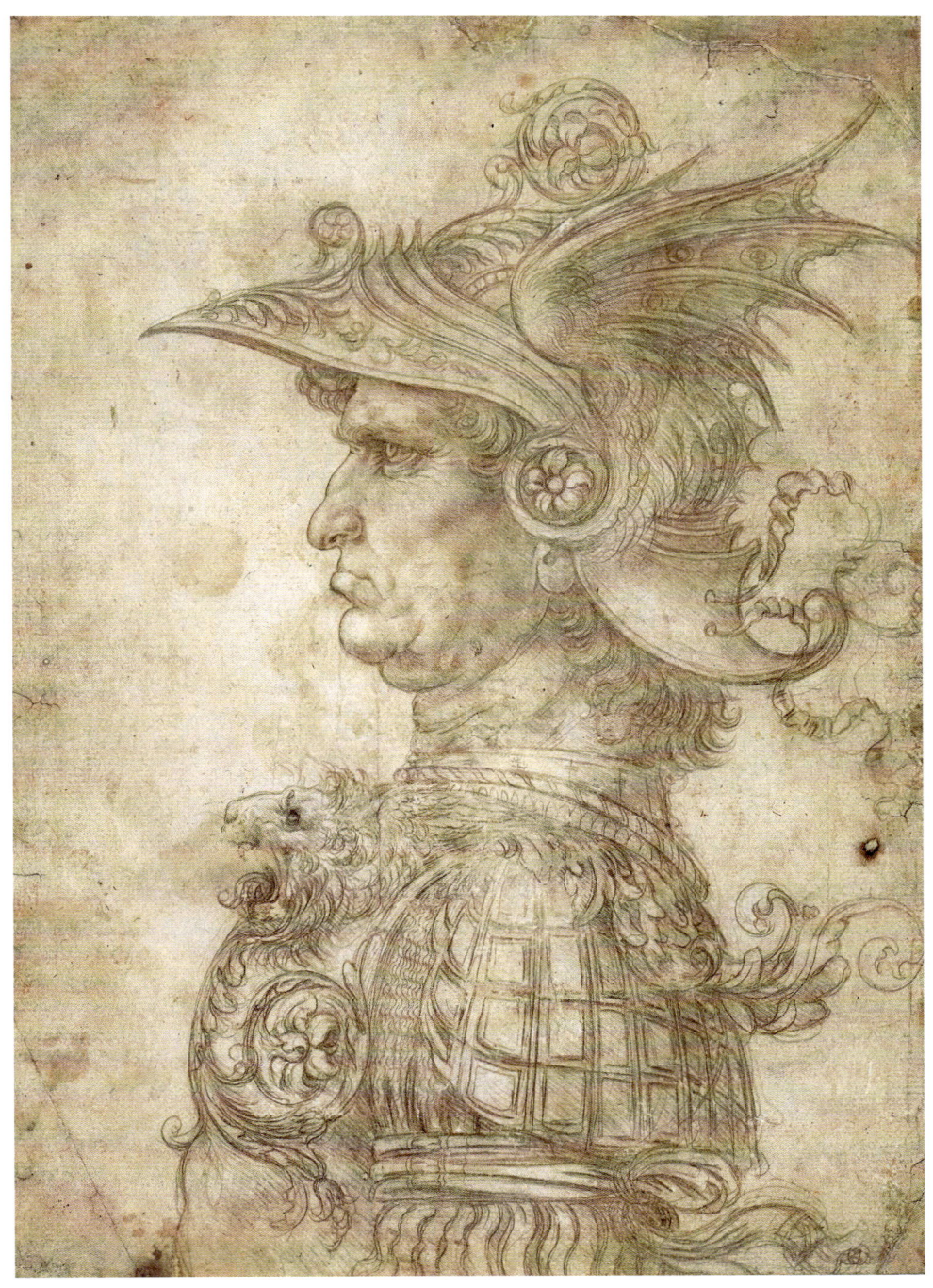

Madonna of the Carnation (Madonna with a Carafe of Flowers), (c. 1472–8?)

Oil (and tempera?) on poplar
62 × 48.5 cm
Alte Pinakothek, Bayerische Staatsgemäldesammlungen, Munich

Of Leonardo's paintings of Madonna and Child, this is considered the earliest. It is the one closest in atmosphere to Florentine painting of the 1460s. The painter's lifelong affinity for dramatic mountainous environs is already apparent. Verrocchio taught Leonardo to draw draperies before he was taught painting. Cloth would be dipped in plaster so it would hold its position for prolonged periods. All his life Leonardo would draw plants for both pleasure and for specific purposes (page 10) and this example is the product of careful study from life. Its deteriorated condition impedes appreciation of the naturalism imbued to the flowers and landscape. The edge of a cloth that was once held by the Madonna's right hand is now invisible. Leonardo's paintings, with their delicate glazes, are easily damaged by overzealous restoration. Another factor is that oil paint undergoes an inevitable and irreversible process called saponification, wherein paint gradually becomes transparent. The use of too much oil by Leonardo has resulted in the unfortunate drying pattern on the Madonna's face. This is the first identified instance of Leonardo's lifelong quest to achieve appealing effects that inadvertently led to technical failure. Given the elementary nature of this error, this painting may belong at the very beginning of Leonardo's career, about 1470.

By the 1880s this painting was owned by a German apothecary, entering the collection of the Alte Pinakothek in 1889. Trimming has reduced the work on the left side. It is related to the *Madonna of the Pomegranate (Dreyfus Madonna)* (c. 1470–2 or later?), now in the National Gallery of Art, Washington DC. That composition may have been invented by Leonardo; the execution is so crude it is usually ascribed to Lorenzo di Credi.

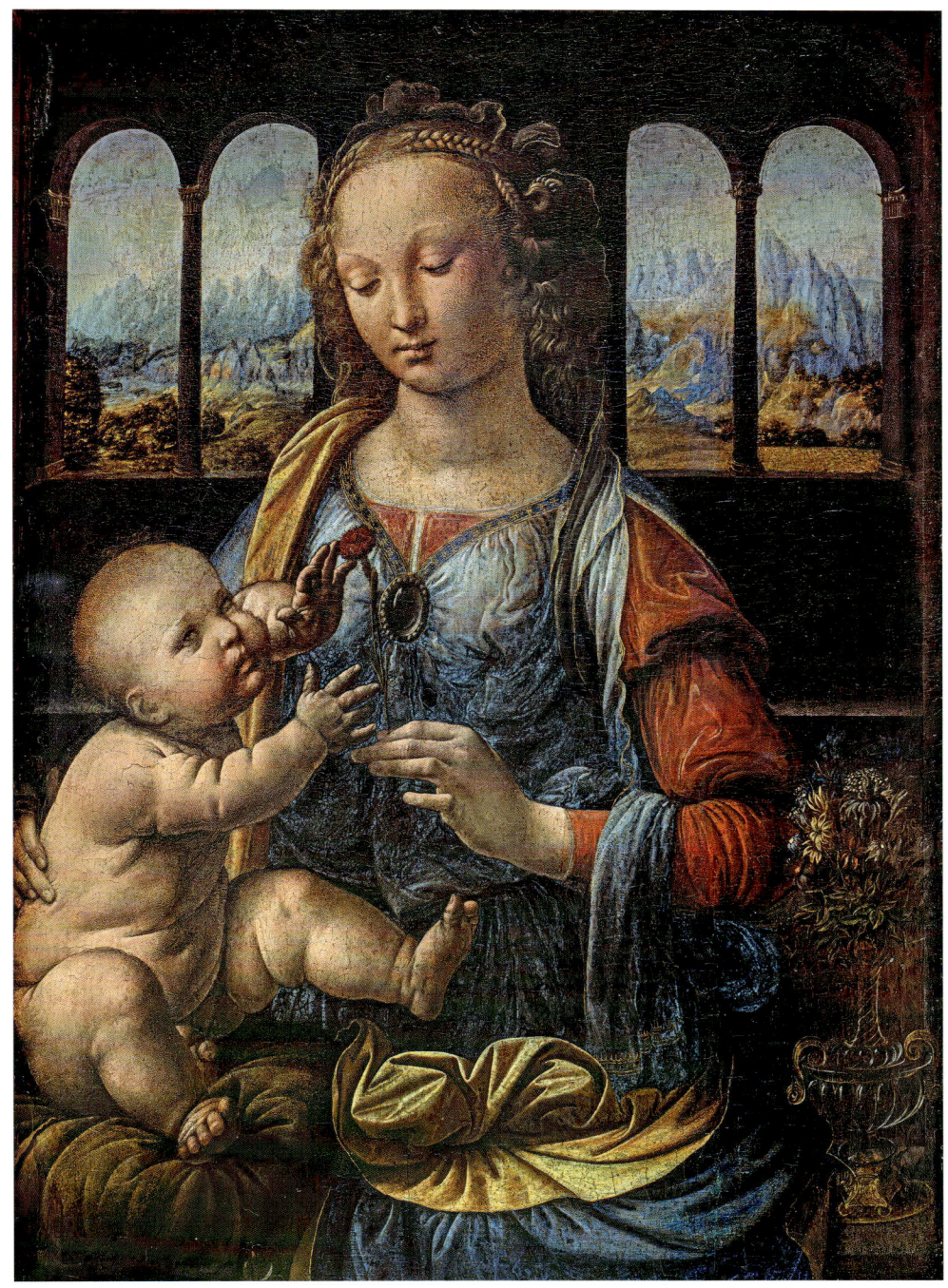

Annunciation (c. 1473–5?)

Oil on poplar
100 × 222 cm
Galleria degli Uffizi, Florence

The Virgin Mary reads at a lectern as the archangel Gabriel appears and announces to her that she will bear the Son of God. Unlike the later *Last Supper* (page 81), the young Leonardo approaches the subject in a conventional manner; the restrained response of Mary reveals nothing of her emotional reaction to such a remarkable annunciation. Beyond the boundary of the garden wall one of the most enchanting views in Western art expands across a wide horizon.

Suffused with a great calm and limpid clarity, this picture is a transitional piece. It exhibits forms and attitudes consistent with Florentine painting of the age, whilst introducing aspects original to the young artist. The treatment of the invented landscape is dense in absorbing detail. The increasingly cool hue, flatness and loss of definition as the topography recedes from us (collectively called "atmospheric recession") derived from Leonardo's observations; it would become a defining characteristic of his painting. The landscape style is Netherlandish in manner, based on the art of the Van Eycks, Petrus Christus and other South Netherlandish masters. We cannot establish what Leonardo might have seen of these paintings, or indeed when.

There are peculiar slips that come with inexperience. The rightmost cypress overlaps the receding wall, making the tree seem oddly small and the wall impossibly massive. The sweet but slightly characterless face of the Virgin and stilted gesture of the angel are imagery borrowed (in spirit if not literally) by a young painter. The foremost wing of the angel was extended by another artist, which has blocked out some of the original landscape.

There is a very simplified version of this *Annunciation*, thought to be by Lorenzo di Credi, on a small panel in the Louvre.

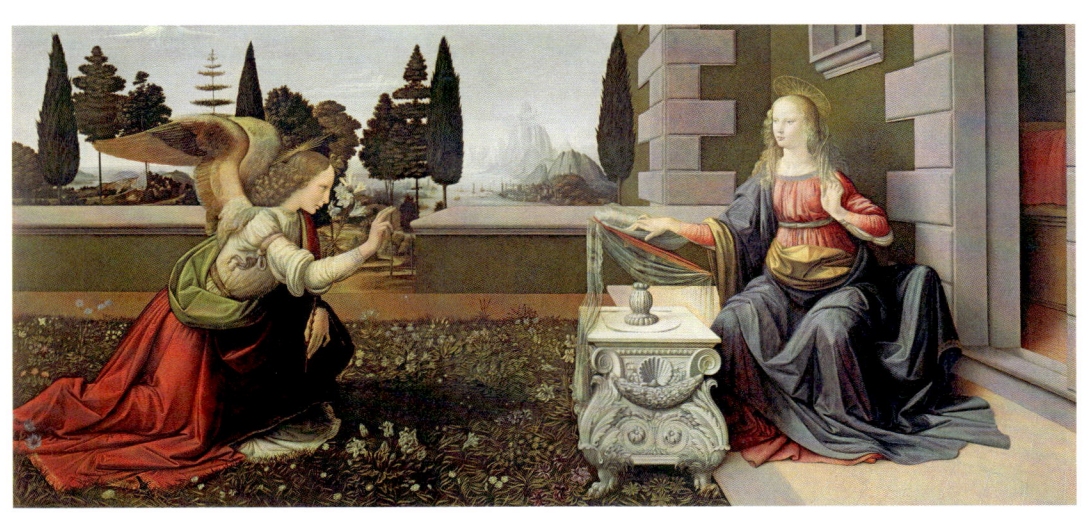

Ginevra de' Benci (c. 1475/1476 or c. 1478–80)

Oil on poplar
38.1 × 37 cm
National Gallery of Art, Washington DC

A pale-faced lady is seated before a dark tree; her face is depicted with gentle shading that brings out a rather chilly elegance absent from Verrocchio's more vivacious portrait bust of her (page 12), discussed below. Although reproduction often flattens the juniper tree, its strong outline and dark mass form an impenetrable barrier between the sitter and the landscape behind, which makes the pictorial space rather awkward to read. Leonardo's unconventional approach to painting can be attested to by the presence of his fingerprint in the juniper foliage, where he manually manipulated paint.
Ginevra de' Benci was the wife of Luigi di Bernardo Niccolini, but the commissioner of this portrait is thought to have been a Venetian diplomat assigned to the Florentine Republic. Bernardo Bembo developed a platonic infatuation with the young Ginevra, who was born in 1457. Bembo was in Florence for two periods: first, January 1475 to April 1476, second, July 1478 to May 1480; the portrait has been dated accordingly. Due to the archaic aspects (flatness of background, stiff posture), the early date seems most likely. This portrait and the Annunciation (page 49) share colouration and handling. The panel has been trimmed on the left and at the bottom, perhaps due to damage at the base. The latter alteration removed the subject's hands. We have a drawing which is thought to be a study of the lady's hands (page 17), showing Ginevra holding a posy. This would match the beautiful bust, carved in marble in Verrocchio's studio. Female portrait busts that include hands are rare in this period. This one was carefully carved on the back, increasing its naturalism.
On the reverse of Leonardo's panel was Bembo's motto "Virtutu[s et] honor" (Latin: virtue and honour), although a later hand adjusted it. Above it is a juniper tree (*ginepro*) encircled by a wreath of laurel and palm, also emblems of Bernardo Bembo.

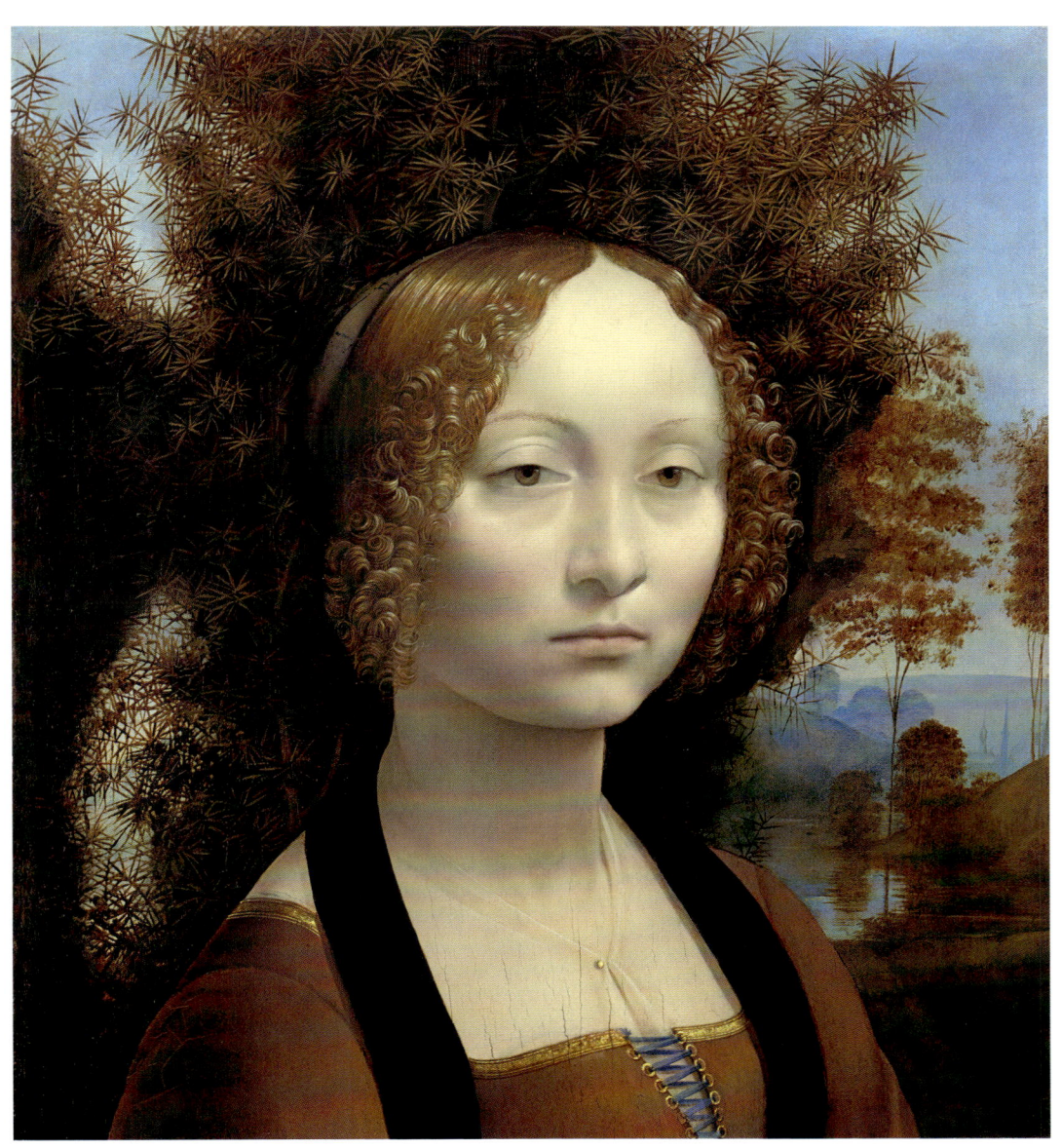

Benois Madonna (c. 1478–80)

Oil on wood transferred to canvas
49.5 × 33 cm
Hermitage, St Petersburg

Although this has been dated as late as 1490, it is possible the *Benois Madonna*
had already been started by late 1478, when Leonardo drew up an inventory which
included two unfinished paintings of the Madonna.

Departing from the common Italian iconography, the Madonna is depicted as a young
(teenaged) woman. She is full of joyous high spirits, entranced by her playful son and
fully absorbed in the moment. Her positioning has a degree of candid verity. She is
not presented to an audience; instead, Leonardo has recreated the natural behaviour
of a loving mother. The infant Christ holds a crucifer flower, symbol of his coming
martyrdom upon the cross.

Sadly, this enchanting painting is seriously damaged and repainted, so it is hard to
appreciate properly. It was in Russian collections from the early nineteenth century
onward, with no explanation as to how it came to be there. The last private owner
of the painting was Léon Benois, who sold it to the Hermitage Museum. When the
Hermitage's restorers removed the painting surface from its panel to attach it to
canvas, a strip 1.5 cm wide was added to the bottom.

In 1485 Leonardo accompanied the Duke of Milan on a diplomatic mission to Hungary.
From the king of Hungary came an order for a Madonna by Leonardo. We do not
know the design of that Madonna, whether it was based on one of these early
Madonnas and why it was never delivered.

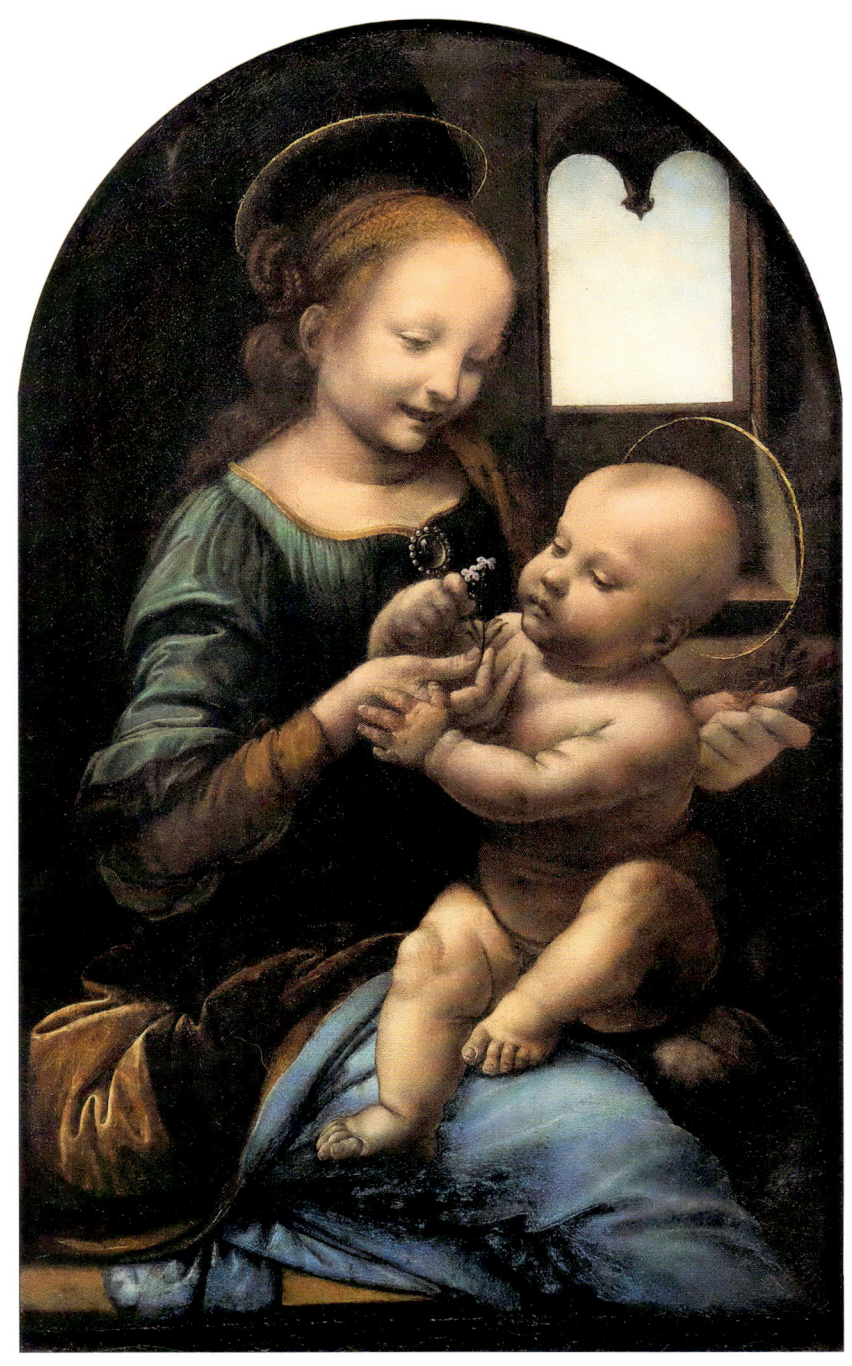

The Adoration of the Magi (1481/2)

Charcoal, ink and oil on poplar
243 × 246 cm
Galleria degli Uffizi, Florence

The iconography of the Adoration of the Magi—when the three kings Caspar, Melchior and Balthasar came to pay homage to the infant Christ—traditionally places the stable and manger on the site of a ruined Roman temple, symbolising the superseding of the pagan era by the Christian one. Although the Adoration of the Magi is usually depicted as having few figures, there is an apocryphal tradition that describes the Magi arriving with extensive retinues, although there is no mention of this profusion of beasts. The soldier on the right looking away from the central group is thought to be a self-portrait. In religious scenes with a large array of characters, artists of this period often included their own likenesses.

For the first time, Leonardo dares to be bold and invent freely. He dispenses with traditional solutions and creates a deep space with multiple incidents unrelated to the central subject. It is his break-through work, as he liberates himself from literal illustration and embraces allusion. "The painter will produce pictures of small merit if he takes for his standard the pictures of others", he commented.

After working on this painting for less than a year, Leonardo declined to finish it, leaving it at the underpainting stage. Recent cleaning has removed varnish and non-original overpainting. It seems Leonardo was sufficiently satisfied by his radical solution and had no interest in completing it. This high-handed attitude was quintessentially modern in its assertion that the artist was a thinker of the liberal arts, not a tradesman of the manual arts. It proved influential perhaps precisely because it was in essence a giant sketch. Application of colour and smoothing of surfaces would have concealed the *Adoration*'s most valuable lesson for artists: that painting can include the genesis of its own creation process as a part of its finished state.

The disgruntled monks never received the panel for which they had paid Leonardo. His painted sketch was left in the care of Giovanni de' Benci, brother of Ginevra and later came into the possession of the Medici, before it entered the Uffizi Gallery.

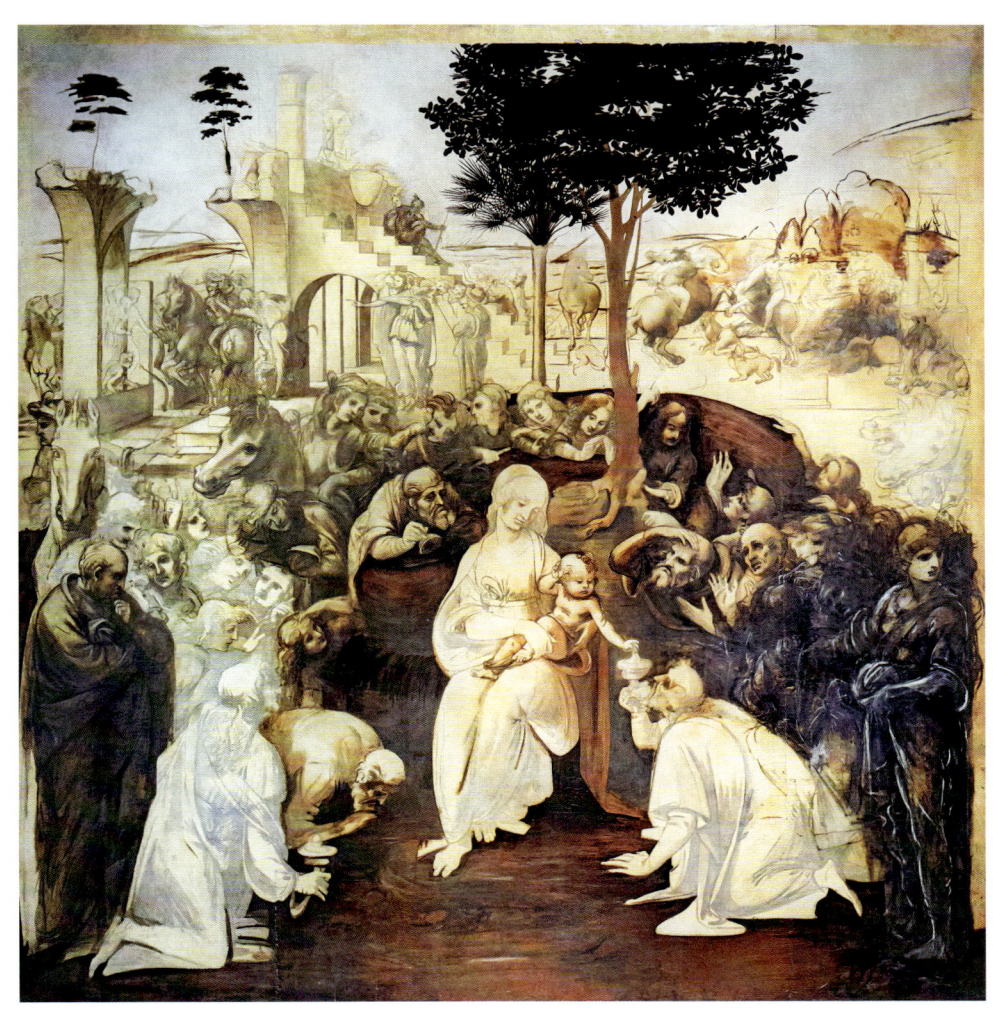

The Virgin of the Rocks (1483–5)

Oil on wood transferred to canvas
199.5 × 122 cm
Musée du Louvre, Paris

On 25 April 1483 Leonardo signed a contract with the Confraternity of the Immaculate Conception of the Blessed Virgin Mary to provide an altarpiece destined for the Church of St Francesco Grande, Milan. He would be assisted by Ambrogio de Predis (c. 1455–1508) and Evangelista de Predis (1440–1490), two brothers of a family of artists. Leonardo lodged with them during the beginning of his time in Milan. Two musician angels on the wings of this panel are considered the handiwork of the Predis brothers. It was stipulated that the central panel be the work of the Florentine, painting in oils. The subject—which appears nowhere in the Bible but is an amalgamation of apocryphal stories—depicts the Rest on the Flight into Egypt. The Holy Family fled King Herod's wrath and *en route* sheltered in a cave; there took place an Adoration of Christ by the infant St John the Baptist, accompanied by archangel Uriel. St Joseph, whom viewers would have expected to see present, is absent. Was the painter perhaps asking us to see the scene through the eyes of St Joseph?

We are caught by the interplay of light hands against the dark background, as they reveal the moods and intentions of their gestures. The care lavished on the botanical details in the foreground springs from Leonardo's lifelong love of plants, which he drew for reference, instruction and pleasure (page 10). The atmosphere of this painting was original and unusual in its day. It has a hushed feeling because of its almost subterranean setting. Just as one enters a gloomy enclosed space after being out in bright daylight, our eyes need time to adjust in order to perceive the muted colours. The theatrical treatment of illumination anticipates the approach of Caravaggio, who greatly admired Leonardo.

This painting soon left the church. It may have been acquired by the Duke of Milan and given as a wedding gift to the Holy Roman Emperor Maximilian. It was later given to the French king as a diplomatic gift.

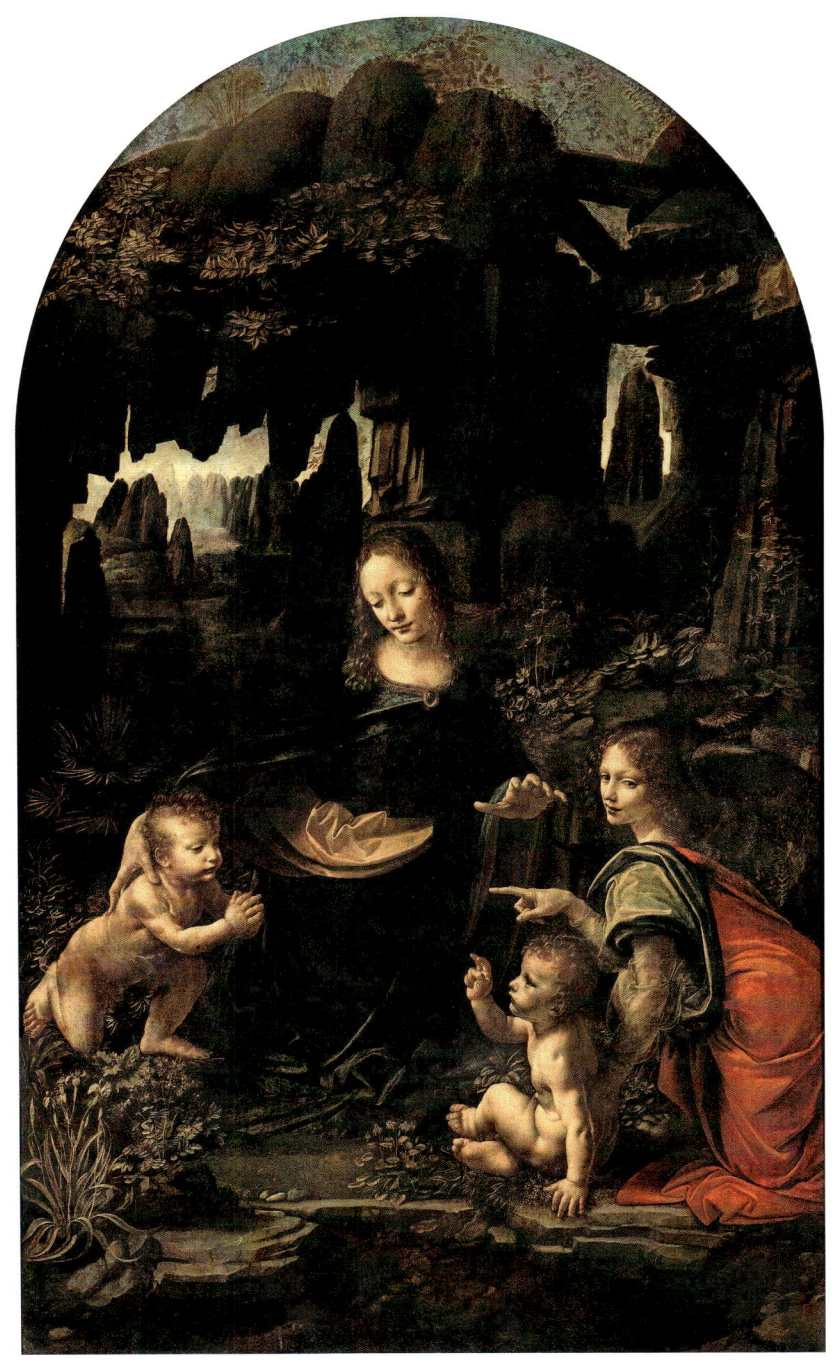

Portrait of a Musician, (c. 1485)

Leonardo da Vinci (and Giovanni Antonio Boltraffio?)
Tempera and oil on wood (walnut?)
44.7 × 32 cm
Pinacoteca Ambrosiana, Milan

The nature of this portrait was unknown until the early twentieth century, when cleaning revealed traces of musical notation and the inscription "Cant. Ang." on the paper. From that we surmise this is a musician. It may be Atalante Migliorotti (active c. 1482–1535), supposedly Leonardo's music teacher and his companion when he moved to Milan. Aside from the possibility that this was a ducal commission, the portrait might be a testament to a personal friendship between musician-instrument maker and musician-painter.

Although Leonardo loved music, he declared painting "ranks higher than music, because it does not fade away as soon as it is born …. It endures and has all the appearance of being alive, though in fact it is confined to one surface. Oh wonderful science which can preserve transient beauty of mortals and endow it with a permanence greater than the works of nature".

Kemp wrote of this portrait, noting it "vibrates with at least some measure of inner life characteristic of Leonardo's autograph paintings. The nervous energy of the bony face and intensity of the intelligent eyes lie outside the reach of even his best followers". The sumptuous curls are painted with a skill we recognise as Leonardo's. The harshness of the face may be due to an absence of a final softening layer of glaze and seems to match the style of Giovanni Antonio Boltraffio (1467–1516), who was one of Leonardo's most able assistants. The unfinished appearance of the tunic may be misleading. It has been suggested that this is an instance of Leonardo using a rough application to not distract us from the face and hand of the subject. This approach was a favourite one of Velázquez and (subsequently) Goya and the Impressionists, who followed Velázquez. My personal view is that the painting is simply incomplete.

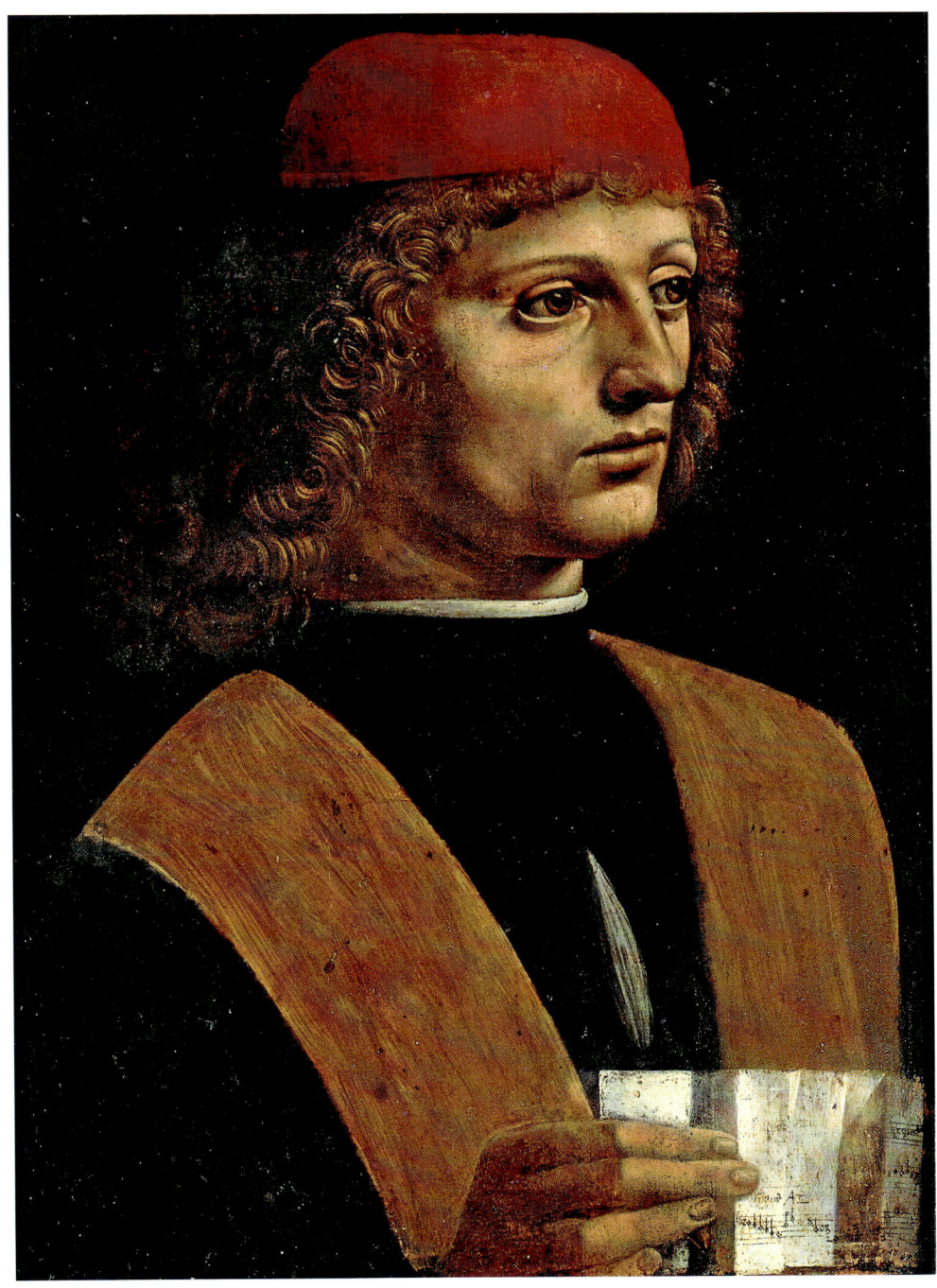

Study for the Head of a Girl (c. 1488–90)

Silverpoint on prepared brown paper
18.1 × 15.9 cm
Biblioteca Reale, Turin

Related to archangel Uriel in *The Virgin of the Rocks* from 1483 (page 57), this study of a female head may have been made after that painting, rather than in preparation for it. A putative date of c. 1490 makes this drawing too late as preparation for the first version and too early as preparation for the second, not started until around 1495 (page 77). It most closely resembles the first version's archangel. As ever, Leonardo's art—that is not related to a datable visit or a commission contract—renders dating difficult.

The drawing is executed in silverpoint. The technique of metalpoint requires a surface to be prepared with gesso (a mixture of glue and chalk or plaster), a wire or sharpened point can be scratched over it. The resultant trace darkens as it oxides; it is permanent and not correctable. Silver was the most common metal but gold and lead were also used. Metalpoint drawings were widespread until the late Renaissance, when they were superseded by chalk, ink and (later) graphite.

Before paper became more common and affordable, metalpoint was the preferred technique on prepared panels that would be resurfaced. Drawing was the core of art training. It allowed students to practise observing and recording from life. It was necessary to plan designs, which could be revised by the master or his deputy. Individual drawings were kept loose or bound into copy books, so they could be guides for future students or reused in other projects. These copy books were sometimes passed down through generations and treated as valuable studio working materials.

This beautiful study—which combines carefully modulated volumes and precise shading—manages to retain a certain airiness due to the loose brisk hatching. The shading is left-handed, that is, strokes start at the top left side and move downwards to the lower right side. Some of Leonardo's right-handed assistants mimicked the master's shading, making attribution sometimes difficult.

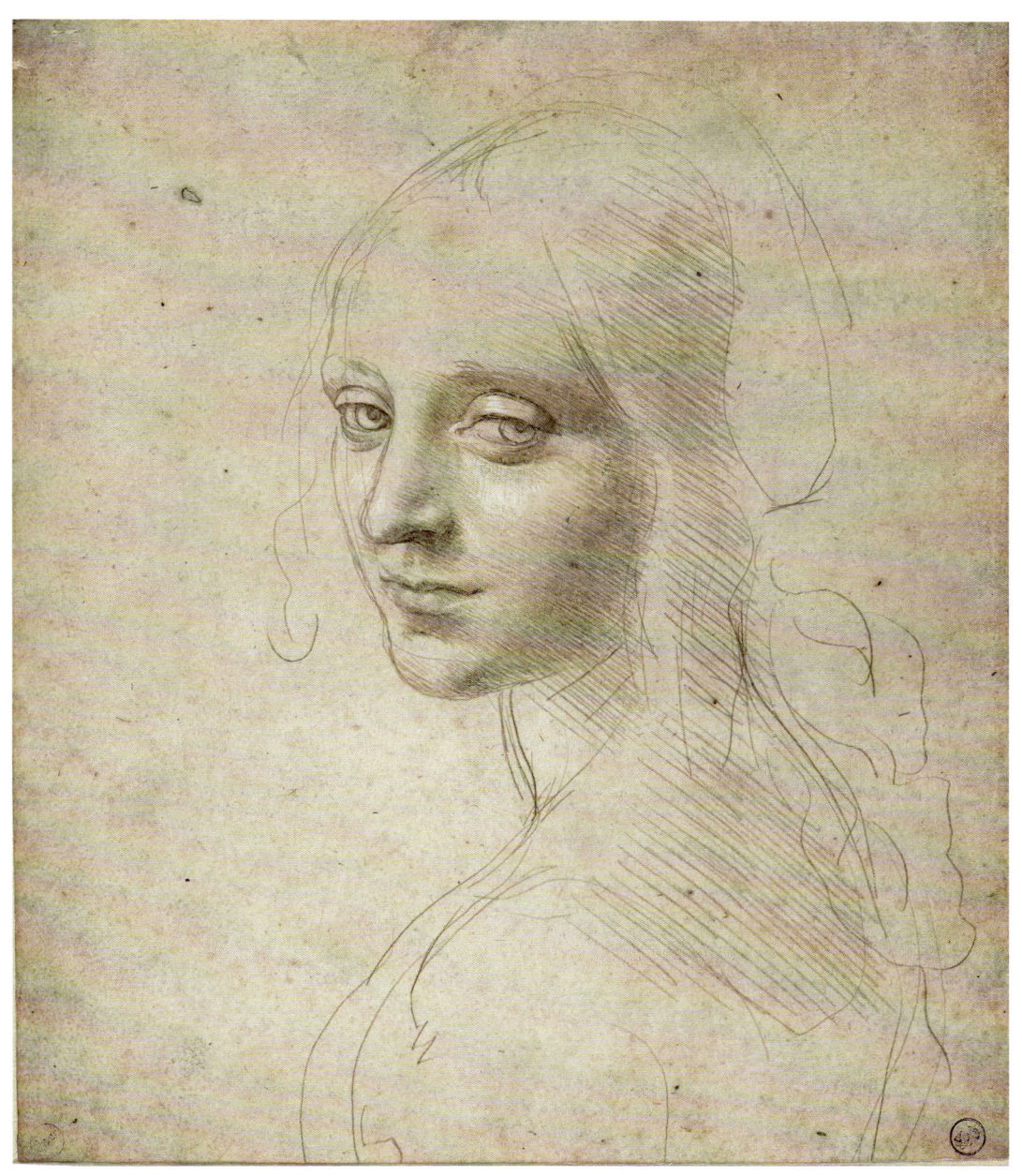

St Jerome in the Wilderness (c. 1488–90?)

Oil and tempera on walnut
103 × 74 cm
Pinacoteca Vaticana, Rome

St Jerome was a popular figure for devotional art. He was a scholar and translator of Christian texts who lived in the Roman era. We see him depicted in two settings: firstly, as a wise man clad in cardinal's garb in his study; secondly, as a penitent hermit in the wilderness, sometimes accompanied by a lion, which he had tamed by healing its paw. In this picture, prominent diagonals balance vertical and horizontal lines, centring our attention on St Jerome's face.

We do not know when or for whom this painting was commissioned. We know nothing about its early history and no contemporary documentation has been traced. At some point, the saint's head was sawn from the panel, an injury which has since been rectified. How did St Jerome come to Rome? Was it brought by Leonardo when he moved there in 1513?

Initially, art historians gave an early dating of this painting due to its similarity to the Adoration (page 55), which is known to be early. However, in the light of Leonardo's anatomical drawings, the painter's increasing expertise in anatomy would be reflected in this confident and accurate painting. The picture is on walnut, a wood rarely used for painting in Florence but common in Milan, Leonardo's home from 1482 to 1499. The lightly sketched church in the top right is very similar to a drawing roughly dated 1488–90, which also assists in dating this panel. The painting is in tempera and oil and we know Leonardo used tempera for underpainting panels until c. 1490, as well as for The Last Supper (page 81).

Leonardo would likely have been familiar with a painted head of St Jerome produced in Verrocchio's studio around 1465, which was in the Medici collection. It also exists as a bronze bust and displays similarities to Leonardo's later conception.

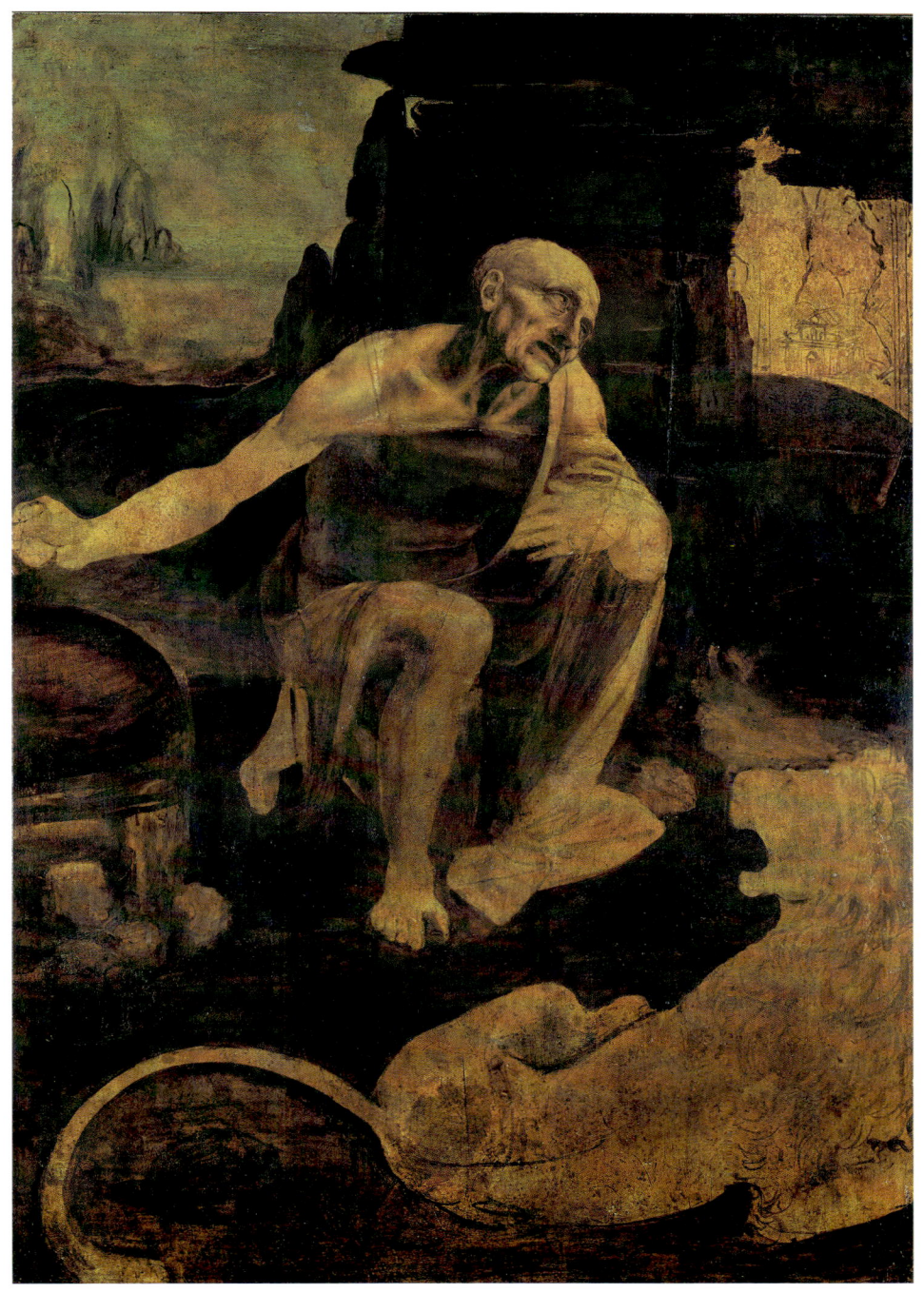

Cecilia Gallerani (Lady with an Ermine) (c. 1489/90)

Oil on walnut
55 × 40.5 cm
Muzeum Narodowe, Czartoryski Collection, Krakow

The subject of this portrait is Cecilia Gallerani (1473–1536), mistress of the Duke of Milan, who ordered this portrait. Their affair had begun by 1487; around the time of this portrait Cecilia became pregnant with the duke's child and on 3 May 1491 she gave birth to his son. The affair became an impediment to Il Moro's impending political marriage to Beatrice d'Este (1475–1497), so it was ended by early 1491. Cecilia was soon married to a nobleman loyal to the duke. The misleading inscription of "La Belle Ferronière" was applied posthumously.

This painting shows considerable development since the portrait of Ginevra de' Benci (page 51). The complexity, warmth and insight—produced through sustained observation of the real world—are characteristic of Leonardo's ground-breaking fusion of idealism and naturalism.

The untameable stoat (called "ermine" when in its white winter pelt) is larger than it would have been in life. Its docility here demonstrates the notable charms of the sitter. The ermine was associated with purity. Leonardo noted, "The ermine will rather die than besmirch itself". The animal was believed to be an auspicious one for pregnant women, warding off evil.

Leonardo's decision to use *contrapposto* (It: counterpoise) for twisting movement in subject and animal imparts a life-like quality that accuracy alone cannot. The glimmerings of reflection in the eyes prompt an immediate response from the viewer—they believe they are in the presence not of a representation but of two living beings. *Cecilia Gallerani* has won acclaim as the most enchanting and vivid portrait of a woman made during the Italian Renaissance, surpassing even the *Mona Lisa* (page 87). *Cecilia Gallerani* is more approachable and realistic than the *Mona Lisa*, which is distanced from us by familiarity and its totemic status as a cultural touchstone.

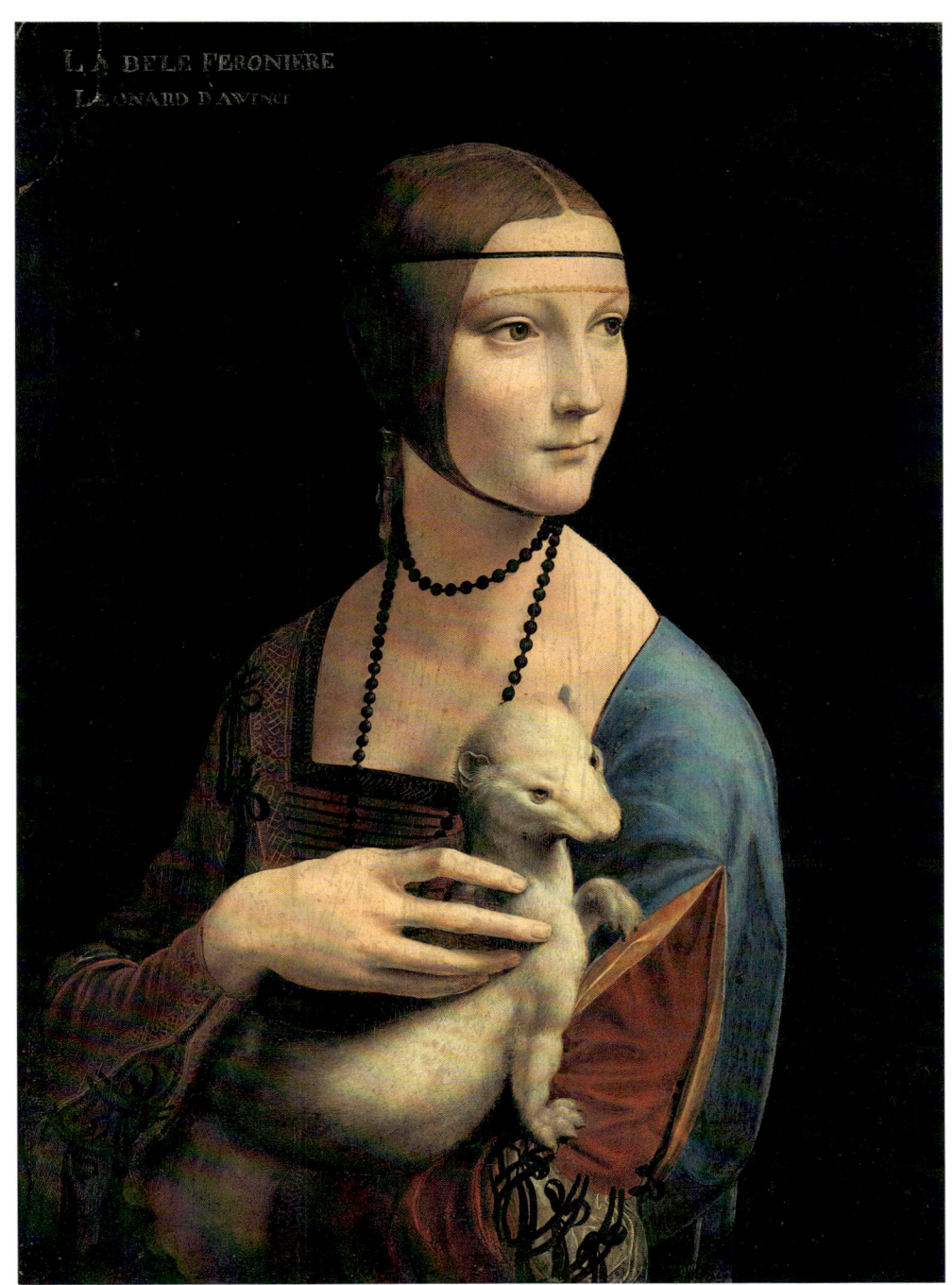

Litta Madonna (c. 1490)

Giovanni Antonio Boltraffio or Marco d'Oggiono (and Leonardo?)
Tempera on wood transferred to canvas
42 × 33 cm
Hermitage, St Petersburg

The Madonna suckles her child, who (in his left hand) holds a goldfinch, a symbol of the Passion. We have a drawing for the head of the Madonna, tentatively dated around 1490 (page 31). That tender sketch—drawn from a live subject—expresses deep calm and profound contentment and is dated around 1488–90; Kemp's dating of c. 1495 seems too late, both stylistically and circumstantially, considering the probable date of this painting, which seems to follow the drawing.

In terms of theme and composition, the *Litta Madonna* is frequently linked to the *Benois Madonna* (page 47) and the *Madonna of the Carnation* (page 46) of the late 1470s, but was probably painted later. It has been attributed to Leonardo, but common scholarly consensus today gives only the design to Leonardo, with the execution being assigned to Boltraffio or another Leonardo collaborator Marco d'Oggiono (c. 1470–1549). Purely in the delicate mountain view do we glimpse something approaching Leonardo's magical subtlety. By the time this picture was produced, he had long ceased painting in tempera (at least as anything other than an underpainting); this fact—plus the style of the modelling of the figures—strongly suggest Boltraffio or d'Oggiono was responsible for the painting.

It is unfortunate that the question of attribution has distracted us from the great beauty and tranquillity of this painting. As is common to Leonardo's compositions, the female anatomy is noticeably inaccurate, with the breast positioned too high. This was done to bring the face of the Madonna closer to Christ, increasing compactness and intimacy.

The painting was in a Venetian collection by at least 1543. Did Leonardo take it to Venice in 1500? It was later in the collection of the Milanese Litta family before being bought by Czar Alexander II in 1865.

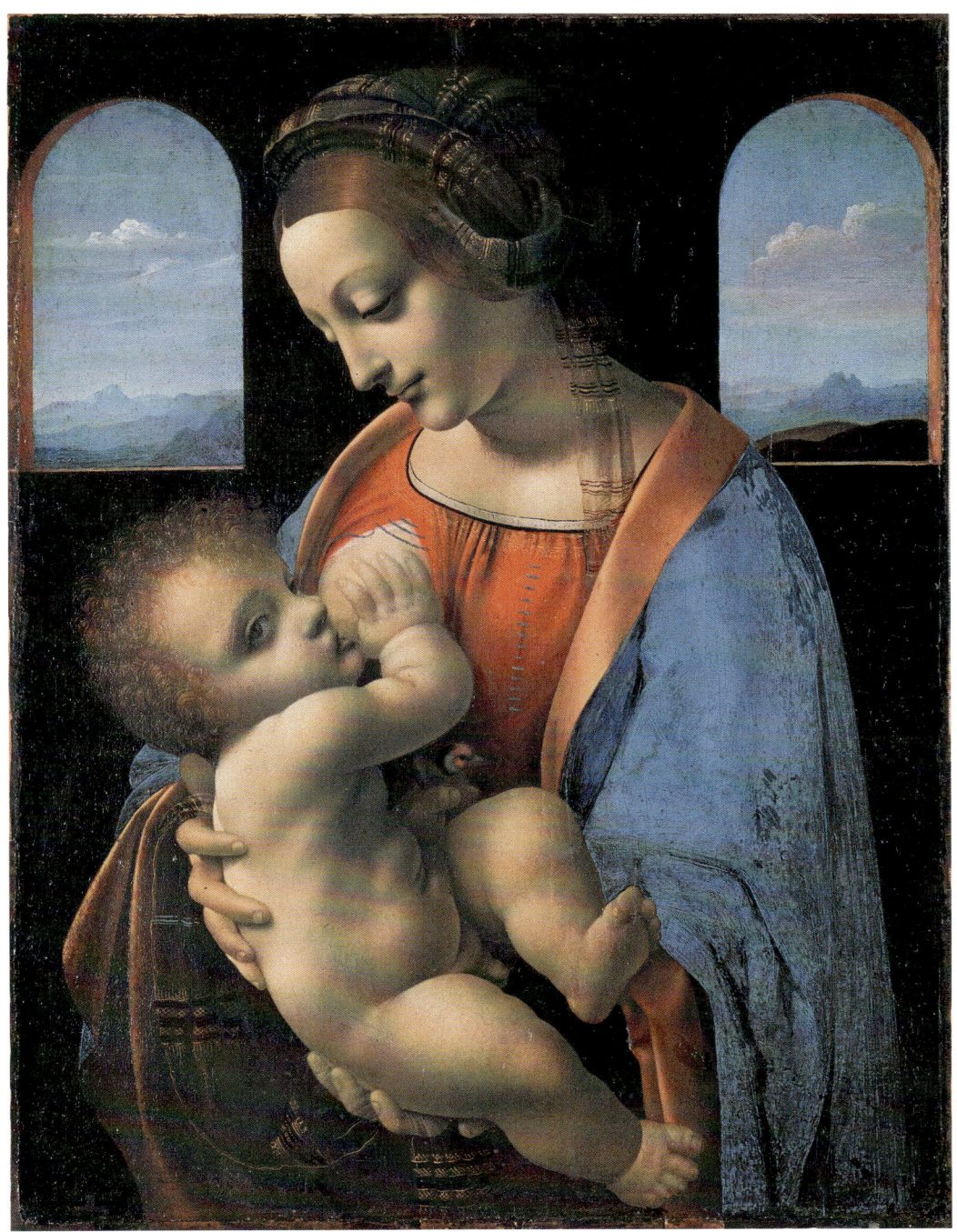

Proportions of the Human Figure (Vitruvian Man) (c. 1490)

Pen, ink and watercolour over metalpoint on paper
34.4 × 24.5 cm
Gallerie dell'Accademia, Venice

De Architectura by the Roman author Vitruvius (c. 80–20 BC) is the only treatise on art and architecture to survive from antiquity. In it, Vitruvius gives ideal proportions for buildings and draws analogies between the human body and the perfect building. As many ancients did, Vitruvius sought ratios that remained constant in microcosm and macrocosm and that could explain divine creation through harmonies of mathematical constants in the physical world—such as the body of man, the solar system, etc.—and abstracts—such as the separations between musical notes and recurring geometrical patterns. An unillustrated edition of *De Architectura* was published in 1486, which Leonardo would have seen, even if he could not have followed the Latin text. Italian versions were published soon after his death. This drawing made its way to Venice, as the centre of the print trade, and this design was destined for reproduction.

As his basis for this illustration, Leonardo took Vitruvius's comparison between the perfect temple and the body of man. "Similarly, in the members of a temple there ought to be the greatest harmony in the symmetrical relations of the different parts to the general magnitude of the whole. Then again, in the human body the central point is naturally the navel. For if a man be placed flat on his back, with his hands and feet extended, and a pair of compasses centred at his navel, the fingers and toes of his two hands and feet will touch the circumference of a circle described therefrom. And just as the human body yields a circular outline, so too a square figure may be found from it. For if we measure the distance from the soles of the feet to the top of the head and then apply that measure to the outstretched arms, the breadth will be found to be the same as the height, as in the case of plane surfaces which are perfectly square."

The perfection of the figure's physique and the care taken to balance linear clarity and pictorial shading elevates this drawing to the highest level of art. Many see Leonardo in the figure's handsome features and long hair, making this vision of the ideal man actually a self-portrait.

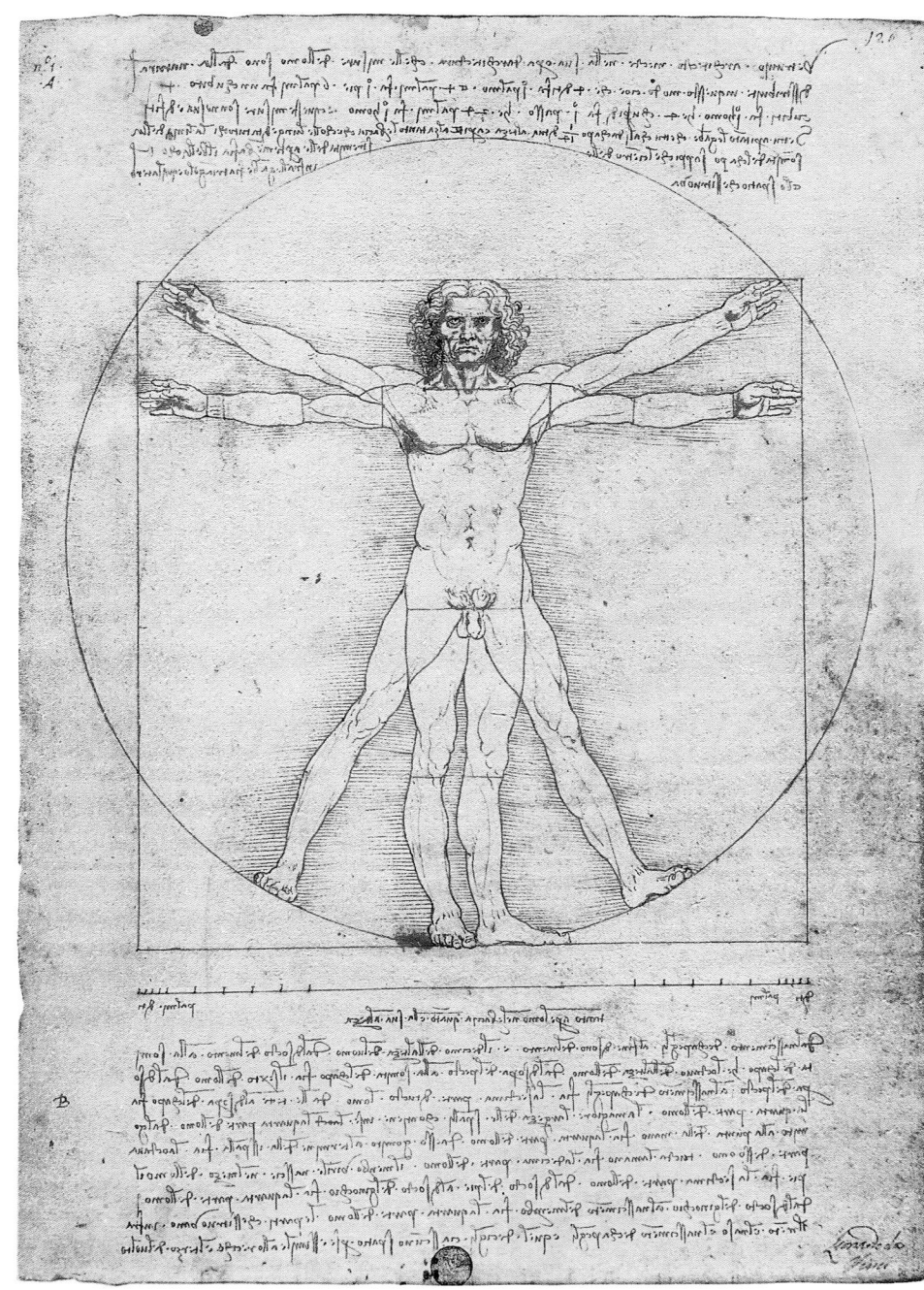

Right Profile of a Horse (c. 1490)

Metalpoint on prepared blue–grey paper
21.4 × 16.0 cm
Royal Library, Windsor

We have numerous drawings made in preparation for Ludovico Sforza's monument to Duke Francesco I, his father. This equestrian statue was entrusted to Leonardo at some time in the 1480s but—according to Leonardo's records—serious work on the project restarted in 1490. Before he constructed wax and clay *modelli*, Leonardo drew horses in the ducal stables, moving around the animals to provide multiple views of the same positions. He measured horses to establish standard equine proportions. This work must have been very agreeable to Leonardo, for Vasari noted, "Although he possessed, one might say, nothing, and worked little, he always kept servants and horses, in which latter he took much delight".
Leonardo envisaged a rearing horse, which would have entailed the entire (unbalanced) weight resting on two slender legs (page 29). His final design was to have three legs on the base and the statue was to be over seven metres high and placed on a tall plinth. The full-size model of the horse, apparently without rider, was unveiled in November 1493 to great acclaim.
"Being of so great a size, an incredible difficulty was encountered in seeking to cast it in one piece", observed Vasari. The sculptor had to develop new systems to overcome the formidable challenges in casting such a huge bronze sculpture. To this end, Leonardo quizzed foundry masters and recalled Verrocchio's system. He filled books with formulae, calculations, costings and diagrams, exploring how to cast a monumental bronze.
In January 1494 war broke out, delaying construction. Eventually, the bronze earmarked for the statue was sent to Ferrara to make cannons. The still uncast clay *modello* was destroyed around 1500 by the French forces that occupied Milan; crossbowmen used the giant horse for target practice.
The scheme of a bronze horse and rider—albeit somewhat smaller—was revived when Leonardo returned to Milan. He envisaged a horse and rider trampling a prone soldier as a monument to Marshal Trivulzio, French-appointed governor of Milan. Drawings were made from around 1508 to 1511 but never reached an advanced stage.

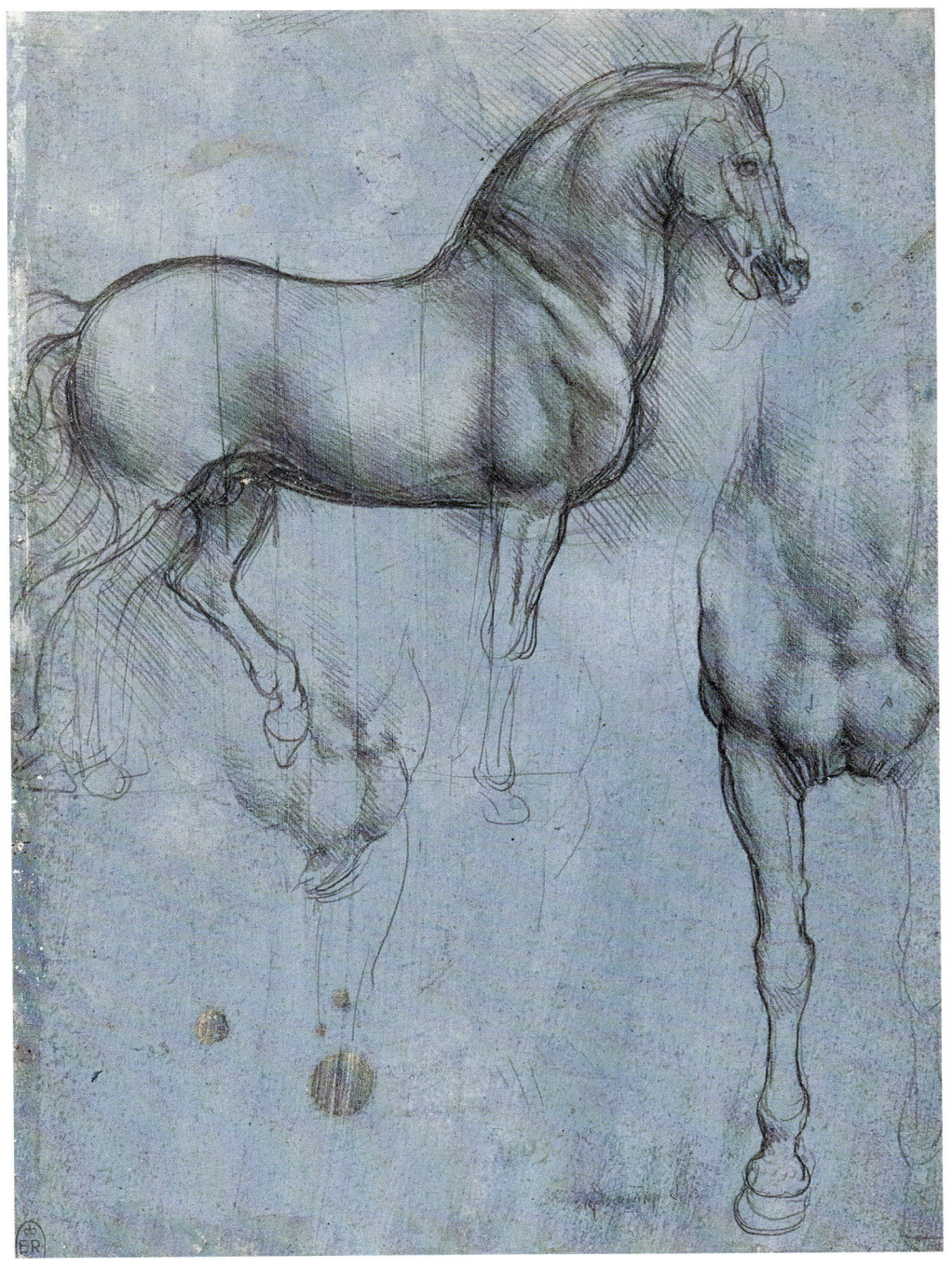

Man Tricked by Gypsies (c. 1493?)

Pen and ink on paper
26.0 × 20.5 cm
Royal Library, Windsor

Martin Clayton (Head of Prints and Drawings for the Royal Collection Trust at Windsor Castle) proposed the current title of this drawing. A man has his fortune read by the woman on the right, while the woman on the left—wearing a gypsy headdress— picks the man's pocket. The moral is that the central figure has been foolishly gullible. Suspicion of gypsy trickery was widespread; in 1493 the duke banished them from Milan. According to Vasari, Leonardo "was so delighted when he saw certain bizarre heads of men, with the beard or hair growing naturally, that he would follow one that pleased him a whole day, and so treasured him up in idea, that afterwards, on arriving home, he drew him as if he had had him in his presence. Of this sort there are many heads to be seen, both of women and of men". Leonardo was fascinated by humanity and a part of understanding the spectrum of human experience is looking at its extremities. He drew labourers and soldiers, whose bodies were in peak condition, and also people with terrible deformities. For Leonardo, prolonged observation of mankind allowed an artist to invent angels and cripples.

Physiognomy—the study of how physical appearance (especially the face and head) relates to behavioural traits—was taken seriously on a wide scale until the twentieth century. Many of us have internalised a liberal worldview so completely that we cannot believe physical appearance indicates character. Although we think of Leonardo as intellectually modern, he had many pre-modern assumptions. We must understand him as a man of his era, not as a modern liberal. For Leonardo and contemporaries, outer appearance betokened inner qualities. Refusing (as a matter of principle) to associate the two would have seemed puzzling and counter-intuitive to them.

Leonardo's grotesques were extremely influential in the sixteenth century, especially with artists from Northern Europe. His drawings of individuals with ugly or unusual features (observed, invented and exaggerated) fit very well to similar physiognomies depicted by Bosch, Grunewald and Massys. Much later, British artist Mervyn Peake successfully took up Leonardo's exaggerated physiognomies in illustrations of Romantic poetry and his own Gothic novels.

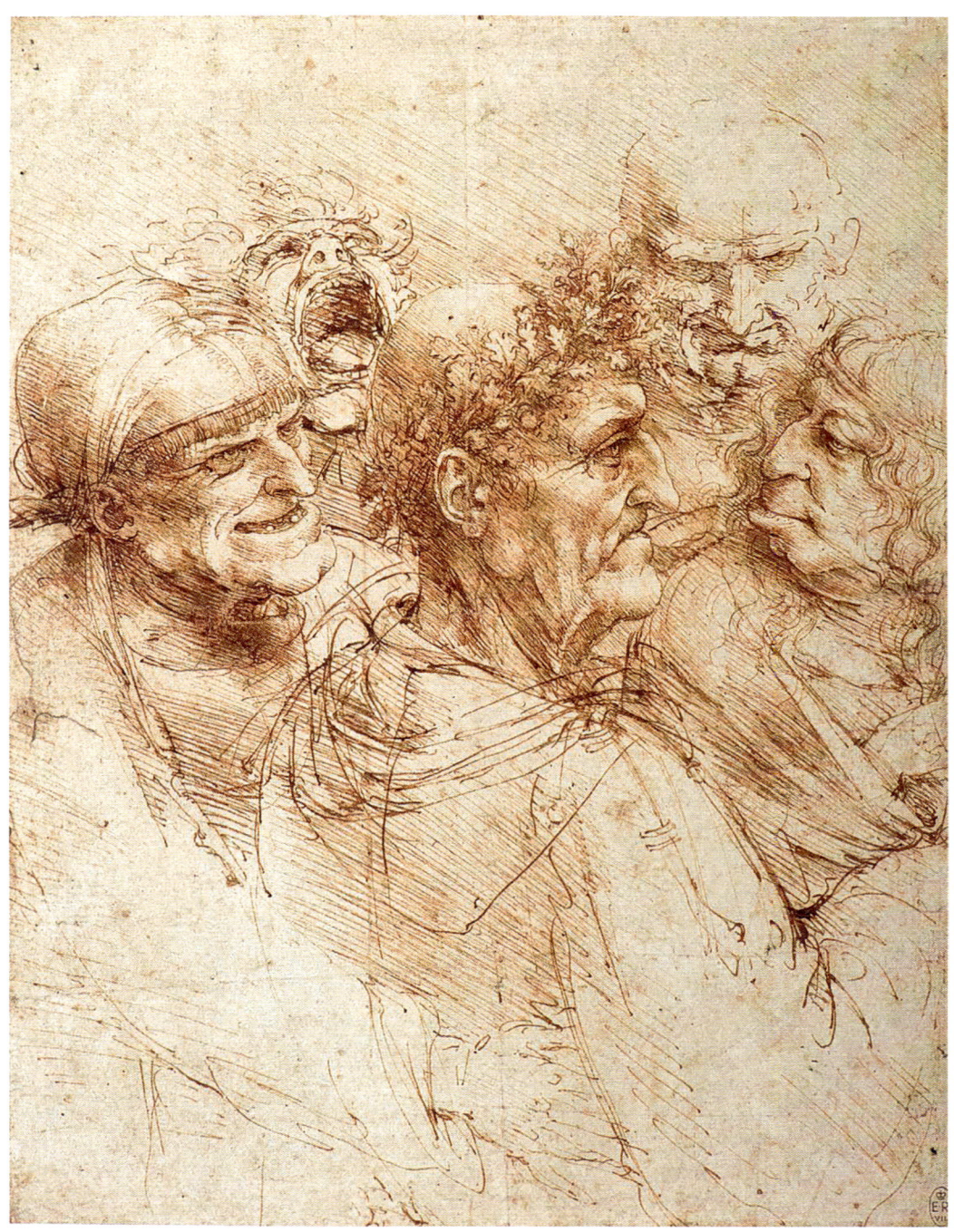

La Belle Ferronière (c. 1490–95)

Oil on walnut
63 × 45 cm
Musée du Louvre, Paris

"The Lady's name is Lucrezia to whom the gods gave all things lavishly. Beauty of form was bestowed on her and Leonardo painted her. Il Moro loved her; one is the greatest of painters, the other of princes. By this likeness the painter roused the jealousy of nature and of goddesses on high."

So wrote an anonymous poet at the Sforza court. *La Belle Ferronière* was made during Leonardo's first Milanese period and the likely subject is Lucrezia Crivelli (1464–1534), as described in the poem. A Milanese noblewoman and mistress of Il Moro, she would give birth to his son in 1497. There is confusion about the meaning of the traditional title of this painting, suggesting the lady was related to an ironmonger (Fr. *ferronnier*). It is actually derived from the band on the sitter's forehead, which is called a *ferronière*, fashionable in Milan at this date.

The subject engages with us by means of her direct gaze. Contrary to Leonardo's satisfaction with solving compositional problems—evident in the unfinished *Adoration* (page 55) and *St Jerome* (page 63)—in his portraits he knew the challenge was mastering a full resolution rather than indicating ideas. Only through perfect finish could his portraits come to life and exhibit the magical lifelike quality that astonished viewers. *La Belle Ferronière* is the perfect demonstration of that; while it lacks the emotional openness of *Cecilia Gallerani* (page 65), it has the presence and gravity of the *Mona Lisa* (page 87), albeit without the latter's elusiveness.

This painting, which is mainly in very fine condition, is of such high quality that we can surmise it is by Leonardo alone, with no visible assistance from the studio. Scientific tests reveal the panel for this picture is probably cut from the same tree that provided the panel for *Cecilia Gallerani*, completed at about the time this portrait was started. Fittingly, this sequence of portraits matches the chronology of the duke's relationships.

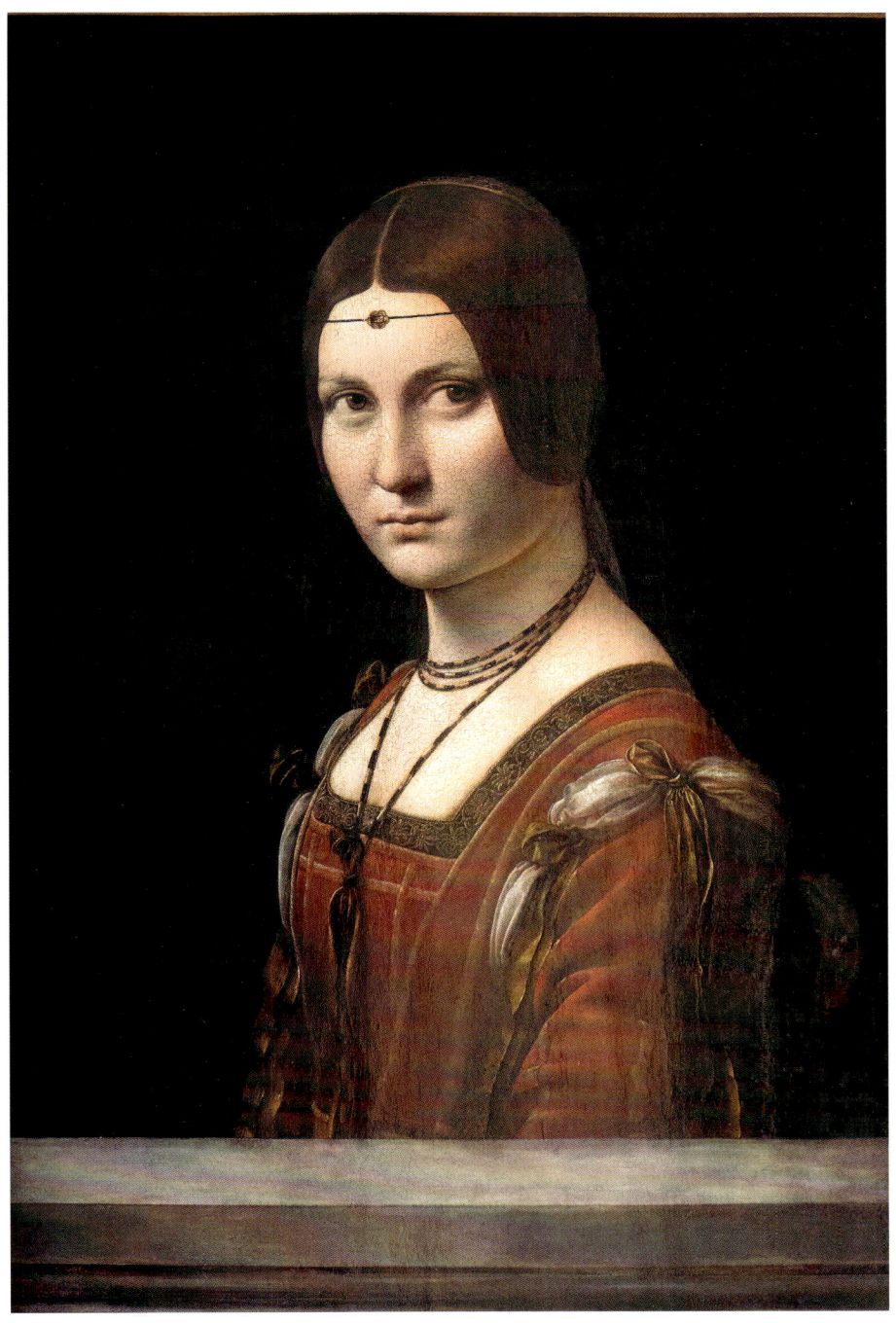

The Virgin of the Rocks (c. 1495–1506/8)

Oil on poplar
189.5 × 120 cm
The National Gallery, London

This painting, made as a replacement for the first altarpiece (page 57), presents a striking dissimilar impression to the earlier version, all the more so considering the compositional revisions are relatively minor. Biographer Charles Nicholl writes of the Louvre version as being warm and crepuscular, while the National Gallery version is cool and nocturnal. The lighting—here much more directional, less diffuse—is not the only difference. The angel's pointing right hand has gone; a cross has been placed beside St John; haloes have been put above the heads of three figures; rocks and plants have been noticeably revised.

Ambrogio and Leonardo submitted legal complaints about late payments for this second painting; the confraternity countered by claiming breach of contract. On 27 April 1506 the verdict went against the painters. The arbitrator stated the product to be deficient—probably an indication that de Predis had painted too much of the central painting of the altarpiece, which was supposed to have been wholly the work of the Florentine painter. This necessitated Leonardo's return to Milan the following month, presumably to correct this deficiency. The handiwork of the master was considered a guarantee of excellence. The contractual phrase "to be painted by the hand of the master" was perhaps more an expectation that the painting would be indistinguishable from the master's best manner, rather than a literal stipulation that only the master himself make the artefact.

Similar to *Leda* (page 36), this painting has been interpreted as an allegory of the mysterious generation of life. Even before his endeavours in anatomical studies of humans and animals, the biology of sexual reproduction had for Leonardo the character of wonderful mystery. He found stories of strange or miraculous conception—found in both Christian teaching and pre-Christian myth—objects of never-ending curiosity. In *Leda* and this *The Virgin of the Rocks*, generation of human life is the subject. In both we witness how new human life is born and consecrated among time-ravaged rocks that will erode and cause—from the resultant dust—plants to grow. The cycle of life—divinely ordained or naturally generated—is a prime concern of Leonardo-as-artist and Leonardo–as–scientist.

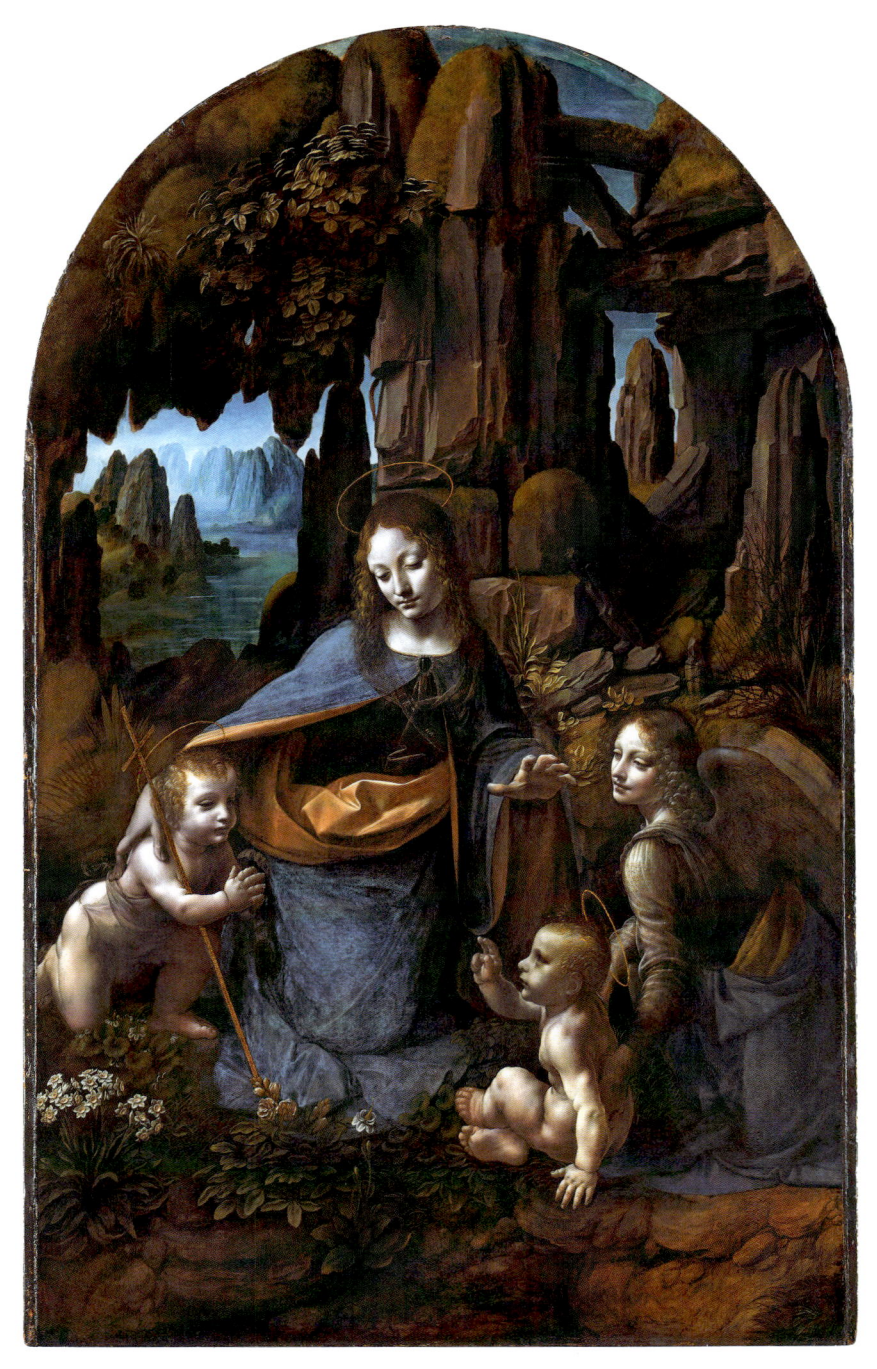

La Bella Principessa (c. 1495/6)

Attributed to Leonardo da Vinci
Coloured chalk with ink on vellum, mounted on board
33.3 × 23.8 cm
Private collection, Switzerland

When it was first documented at the end of the twentieth century, in the possession of a picture restorer, this drawing was considered to be a—possibly nineteenth-century German—pastiche of Leonardo. Recently it has been acclaimed as a Leonardo drawing. Debate about the authenticity of this work shines a light on appreciation for, and imitation of Leonardo. Fascination with *La Bella Principessa* is evidence of our ceaseless desire to find "new" works by Leonardo.

A handful of experts—most prominent among them Martin Kemp—have attributed this drawing to Leonardo. The left-handed shading is consistent with the master's practice, but this was something right-handed artists could have done to emulate Leonardo. The subject is suggested to be Bianca Giovanna Sforza (1482–1496), daughter of Il Moro, not—as sometimes reported—Bianca Maria Sforza, his niece. Supporters of the drawing's status as an authentic Leonardo believe it was made for the opening of the fourth, final volume of a grand illustrated codex called the *Sforziada*, celebrating achievements of the Sforza family, from which a vellum page has been cut out. However, stitching holes at the edge of the vellum of the drawing do not match the stitching of the volume. Scientific examination for fingerprints and DNA linked to the artist have produced results that are contested.

The combination of media—as well as the use of pastel and of vellum—is not seen anywhere in the corpus of Leonardo. As pastel is a completely unsuitable medium for a book illustration (it is very delicate and liable to rub on to the facing page) it is never used for such purposes. Although Leonardo experimented with mediums, he wanted permanence; it is inconceivable he would have chosen such a fragile material for the page of a book. Ambrogio de Predis's book pages are tempera on vellum. It is improbable that an important drawing such as *La Bella Principessa* by a celebrated artist would not have had an inscription nor be commented upon by contemporaries. With the exception of *Bust of a Warrior* (page 45), we do not have any highly finished drawings we could call presentation drawings—intended to be complete in themselves and to be appreciated as individual works of art. Along with many Leonardo scholars, I do not consider this drawing an authentic work by the artist.

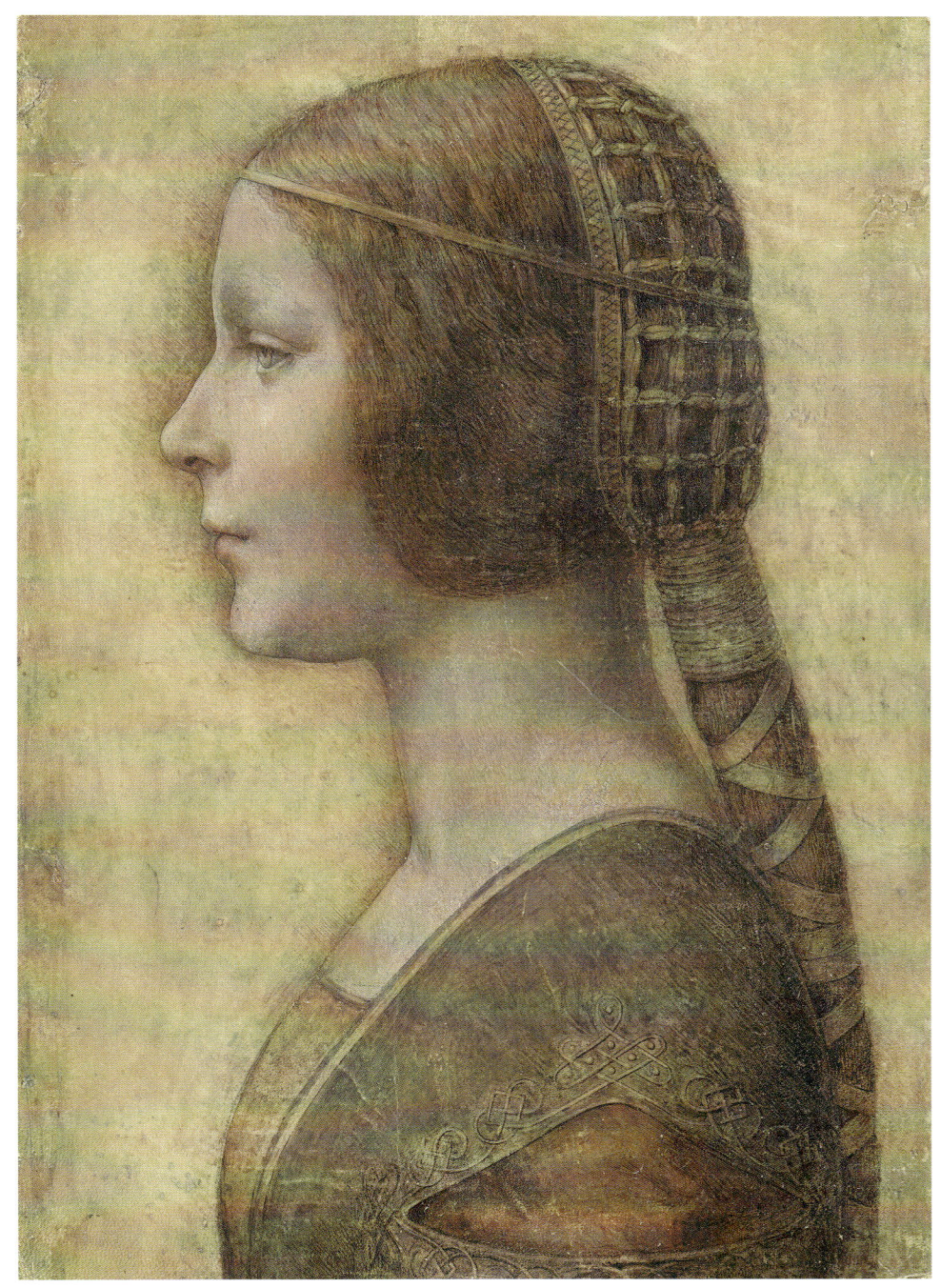

The Last Supper (1495–7)

Tempera and oil on plaster
460 × 880 cm
Santa Maria delle Grazie, Milan

Il Moro, who was a donor to the Dominican monastery of Santa Maria delle Grazie, requested Leonardo decorate a wall of the monastery refectory. Leonardo depicts the moment when Christ tells the Disciples that one of them will betray him. For the first time in art, a painter applied physiological insight, which resulted in the vigorous animation of the Disciples in a way previously unprecedented in depictions of this scene. Leonardo reminded himself: "One who was drinking and has left the glass in its position and turned his head towards the speaker. Another twisting the fingers of his hands, turns with stern brows to his companions. Another with his hands spread shows the palms, and shrugs his shoulders up to his ears, making a mouth of astonishment…. Another as he turns with a knife in his hand upsets a glass on the table".

Attention was given to geometry as well as physiology. One-point perspective converges on Christ's head; Christ's face and hands form an equilateral triangle at the centre of the picture. Leonardo relinquished realism to make Christ larger than his companions, though unobtrusively. His right hand reaches for the wine; the left— reinforced by his gaze—indicates the bread; both components of the Eucharist. Judas recoils, knocking over the salt cellar. St John— immediately to Christ's right—swoons. Novelist Matteo Bandello observed Leonardo at work. "He would arrive early, climb up on to the scaffolding, and set to work. Sometimes he stayed there from dawn to sunset, never once laying down his brush, forgetting to eat and drink, painting without pause. At other times he would go for two, three or four days without touching his brush, but spending several hours a day in front of the work, his arms folded, examining and criticising the figures to himself."

Leonardo's choice of technique—tempera with oil over a double layer of plaster— proved unstable; paint quickly started to flake. Today *The Last Supper* is a ghostly ruin, made legible through recent restoration (in removeable watercolour) that links to Leonardo's paint, of which only about twenty percent survives. Thankfully, *The Last Supper* was copied many times in its early years, likely because people realised it would soon be unrecognisable.

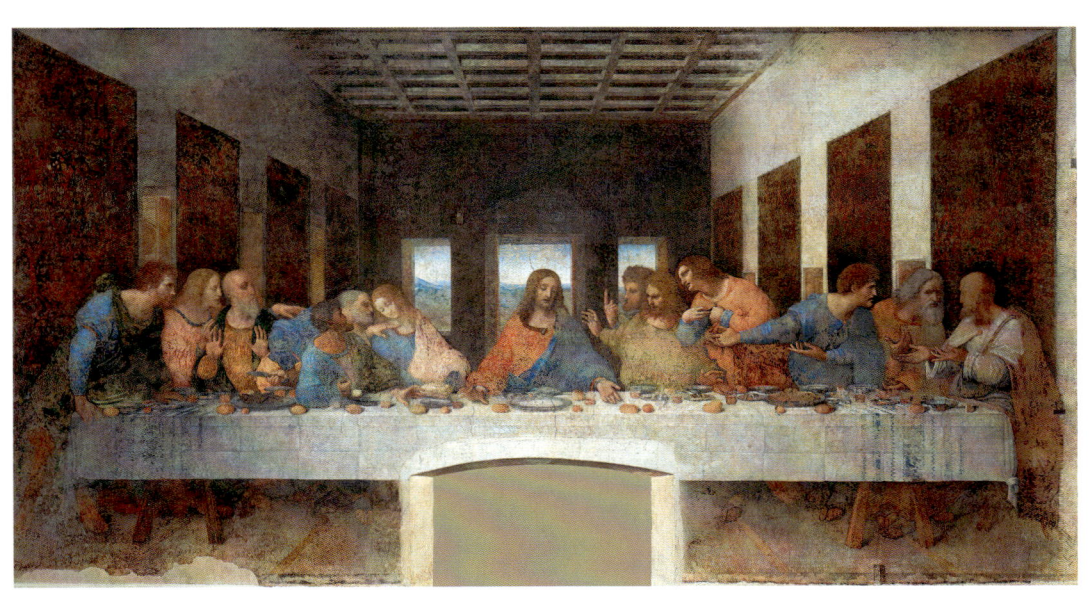

Portrait of a Lady in Profile (Isabella d'Este?) (1499/1500)

Metalpoint, charcoal and white, black and ochre chalks on paper
61 × 46.5 cm
Musée du Louvre, Paris

From December 1499 to March 1500 Leonardo and his retinue were in Mantua. The ruler of Mantua was the Marquess of Francesco Il Gonzaga; his wife Marchioness Isabella d'Este would later rule the Duchy in her husband's absence. Isabella's late sister Beatrice had been married to Ludovico Sforza; she met Leonardo at the Milanese court. Isabella was a committed patroness of the arts and an avid collector of vases, jewellery, statuary, coins and other art, new and ancient. In 1500, the court painter of Mantua was the elderly indomitable Andrea Mantegna (c. 1431–1506). Isabella was set on having her portrait painted by Leonardo. Although he was in need of a patron (or patroness), Isabella was notorious for being controlling and vain. Joining her court would have ended badly for the independently-minded artist. Leonardo extracted himself from Mantua by promising to send a portrait following his departure. Even though we do not have that portrait of Isabella, this cartoon for that portrait is "pricked for transfer". Although the painting was never sent, it was likely started and worked on while Leonardo was in Venice. The description "cartoon" comes from *cartone* (It: large sheet of paper) being a one-to-one scale preparatory drawing of the design for a painting. It is placed over the painting support and transferred by mechanical means, usually the pricking of outlines and the dabbing of powder through the holes, which produces a linear layout of the composition. This drawing has been "pricked for transfer" or prepared for such a use.

Note the position of Isabella's hands, which foreshadows that of the *Mona Lisa* (page 87), to be started three years later. An early copy of this drawing reveals that the parapet on which Isabella's arms rested has been trimmed away. The choice of portrait-in-profile echoes the format of the coins and cameos that Isabella collected.

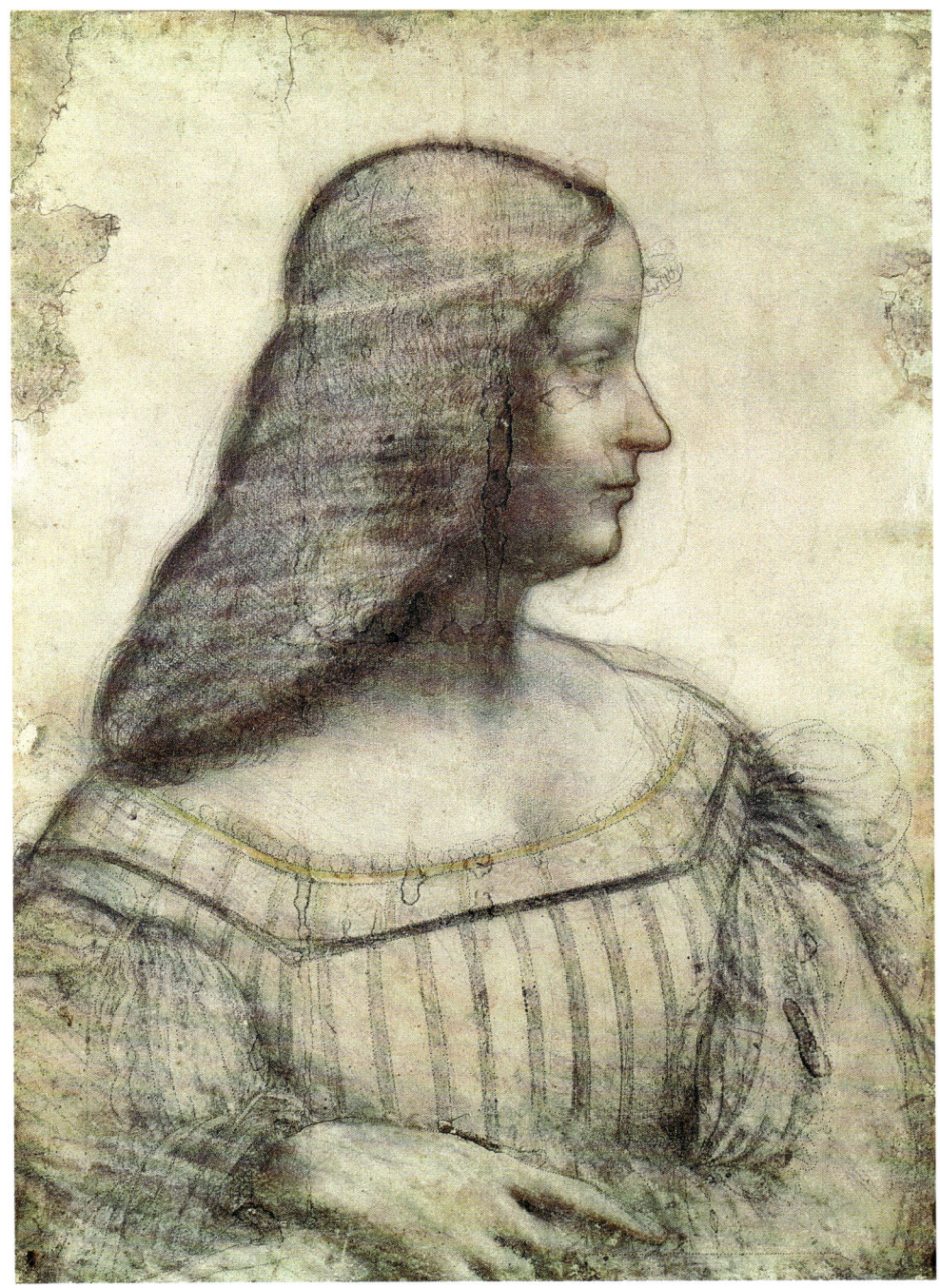

Madonna of the Yarnwinder
(Lansdowne Madonna) (c. 1501–7?)

Studio of Leonardo da Vinci
Oil on wood
50.2 × 36.4 cm
Private collection, New York

This touching tableau situated in a landscape of rocky mountains shows the Christ Child reaching for a yarnwinder, the spindle of which resembles the cross upon which he shall be eventually crucified, with his mother watching on, hesitant and patient. The subtle blending of naturalistic description, religious message and psychological complexity show a marked advance from the sweetness of the *Benois Madonna* (page 53) and the serenity of the *Litta Madonna* (page 67), not to mention the somewhat stilted conventional Maternities by Leonardo's peers.

In a letter of 14 April 1501, a visitor to Leonardo's studio reported, "The little picture he is working on is a Madonna who is seated as if she intended to spin yarn, and the Child has placed his foot in the basket of yarns, and has grasped the yarnwinder, and stares attentively at the four spokes, which are in the form of a cross, and as if he were longing for this cross he smiles and grips it tightly, not wishing to yield to his mother, who appears to want to take it away from him". There is no sign of the basket, but this composition seems authentic, although we have no provenance for it before 1809. Leonardo's original version was reported to be intended for Florimond Robertet, secretary to King XII of France.

There is another version of this composition (the *Buccleuch Madonna*) which also dates from the start of Leonardo's second Florentine period. That painting—about the same size as this—shows mountains adjacent to a lake or sea. Overall, it is harsher in tone, darker in character and the background has been much overpainted. This *Madonna of the Yarnwinder* is in poor condition, due to it being transferred from panel to canvas then back to panel. Kemp believes there was no "original" version, simply these two studio productions. Experts differ regarding how closely Leonardo was involved in the execution of both paintings, although all are unanimous that the composition of the figures is authentic. This painting has been assigned to Salaì or Il Sodoma (Giovanni Antonio Bazzi, 1477–1549).

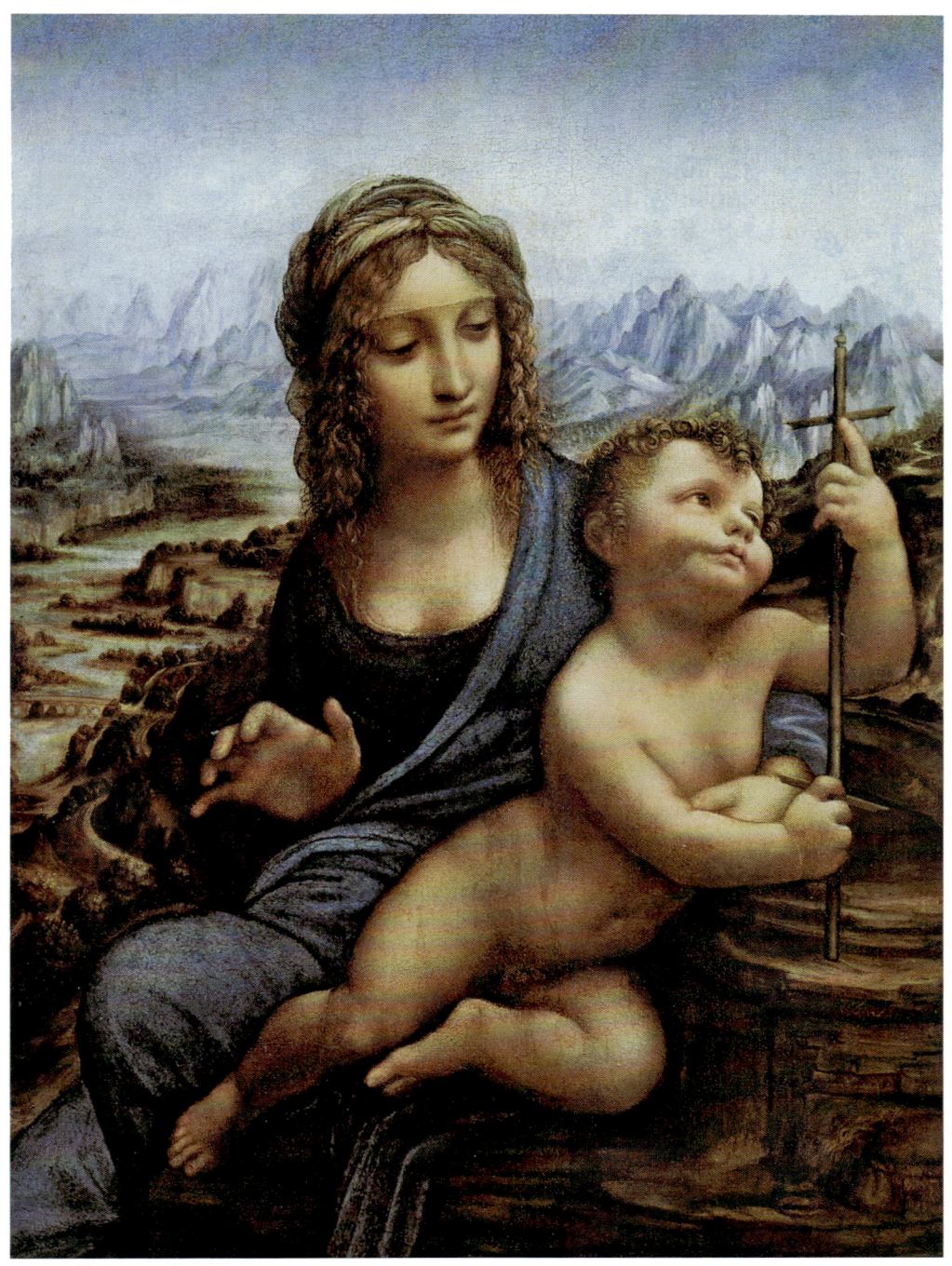

Lisa del Giocondo (Mona Lisa)
(c. 1503–6 and later?)

Oil on poplar
79.4 × 53.4 cm
Musée du Louvre, Paris

Madonna Lisa di Gherardini (1479–1542) was the third wife of Francesco Giocondo, a wealthy Florentine silk trader. Giocondo was known to Ser Piero, who perhaps arranged a portrait commission for Leonardo. The artist had recently returned to Florence and was without a benefactor. Strangely, Giocondo apparently never made any payment for the picture and it was never in his possession. No contract has been discovered nor any related sketches in Leonardo's papers. Even more curiously, when asked about it in 1517, Leonardo apparently said that this portrait was made at the request of Duke Giuliano de' Medici (page 90). Did the writer of this anecdote make an error or was Leonardo misremembering? Why would the duke want this portrait made and for whom was it intended?

The *Mona Lisa* is seen as a distillation of Leonardo's learning in the fields of perspective (aerial recession), optics (*chiaroscuro*), geology (rock formations), hydrodynamics (river) and anatomy in the form of the Mona Lisa herself. Never before had so much care been lavished on modelling a face and capturing the minutest subtleties of physiognomy and expression. There are no hard edges in the picture, which describes volume through shade alone. The painting's softness and richness of colour (muted by discoloured varnish) comes from the use of glazes—small amounts of paint suspended in varnish. The old varnishes cannot be removed due to the fragility of the paint and the danger of removing glazes along with the varnish.

This painting was in the French royal collection and passed to the Louvre. Admired during the mid-nineteenth century, the portrait did not acquire its current fame until 1911, when it was stolen by an Italian labourer doing repairs in the museum. In 1913 it was recovered in Florence and returned to Paris.

Puzzlingly, the painting was described as unfinished during Leonardo's lifetime, yet it is finished and painted solely by Leonardo himself. Around 1505 Raphael made a sketch of the portrait that included pillars. Although the pillar bases can be seen in the *Mona Lisa*, X-rays and paint analysis confirm there never were any pillars; the panel has never been trimmed. Where did Raphael's pillars come from? There seem no end to the riddles that make this iconic portrait mysterious.

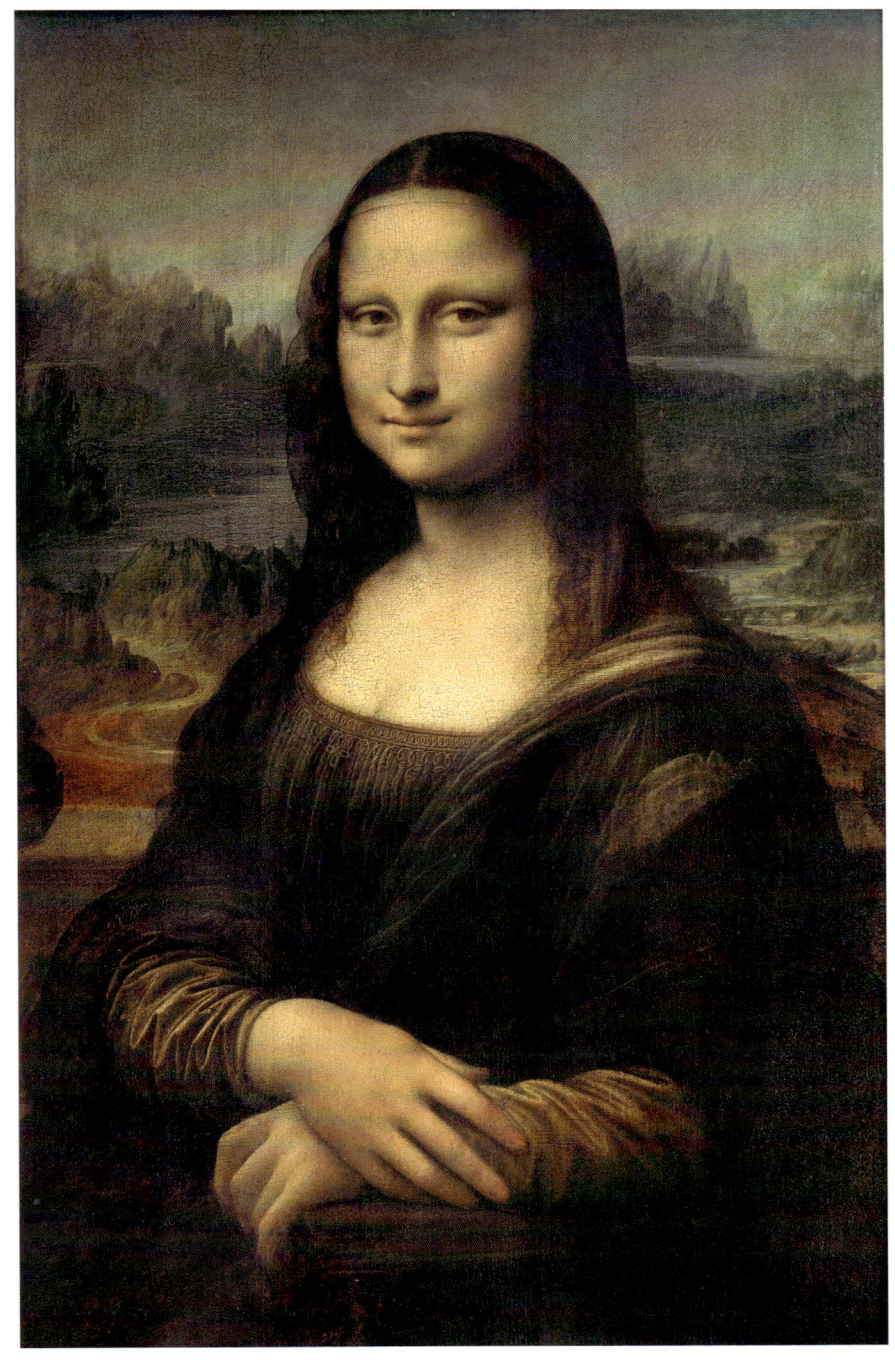

The Battle of Anghiari (copy)
(before 1550 and c. 1603)

Peter Paul Rubens and unknown artist
Black chalk, ink and white lead on paper, reworked with watercolour on paper
45.2 × 63.7 cm
Musée du Louvre, Paris

Work on the design for this mural (on a wall measuring 7 metres high by 17.5 wide) in the Sala Grande of the Palazzo Vecchio, Florence, lasted from 1504 to 1506. Leonardo completed a large cartoon and painted much of this central motif—which consists of the battle for the standard between the Florentines and Milanese—until technical problems with his paint forced him to stop. He wrote of a dramatic incident. "On 6 June 1505, on Friday, at the stroke of the 13th hour I began to paint at the Palazzo. At the moment of putting down the paintbrush the weather changed for the worse, and the bell in the law-courts began to toll. The cartoon broke loose. The water spilled as the jug which contained it broke. And suddenly the weather worsened, and the rain poured down till nightfall. And it was dark as night."

This drawing is not a completely accurate copy. With the soldiers struggling on the ground, the version by Peter Paul Rubens (1577–1640) omits the upper figure about to plunge a stiletto into the throat of the prone man. Copies vary in accuracy. Rubens'—reworked from a drawing by an unknown Italian artist—is not the most literal but it conveys the spirit of the original best. He refined and extrapolated, following his imagination; he never saw the original painting, the remnants of which were covered over in 1572, before he was born.

In an entry from 1490, Leonardo advised painters of battles, "You will give a reddish tinge to the faces, the figures, the air, the musketeers, and those around them . . .. Arrows will be flying in all directions . . .. Men fleeing in rout will be crying out with open mouths. Have all kinds of weapons lying underfoot: broken shields, lances, stumps of swords, and other such things". *The Battle of Anghiari* combined Leonardo's mastery of equestrian art, anatomical studies, weaponry expertise and observations of expressions. The chosen motif was the moment of greatest action and uncertainty, foregoing a scene of patriotic triumph. Leonardo wanted to impress on his audience the fury of war, not least to remind city fathers of their responsibility to conduct the state's affairs prudently.

Following continual speculation about the survival of Leonardo's *Battle* behind a later mural, scientific examinations were undertaken, which were inconclusive. There is no expectation that the Late Renaissance mural (by Vasari) should be destroyed in order to reveal what remains of the surface upon which Leonardo painted.

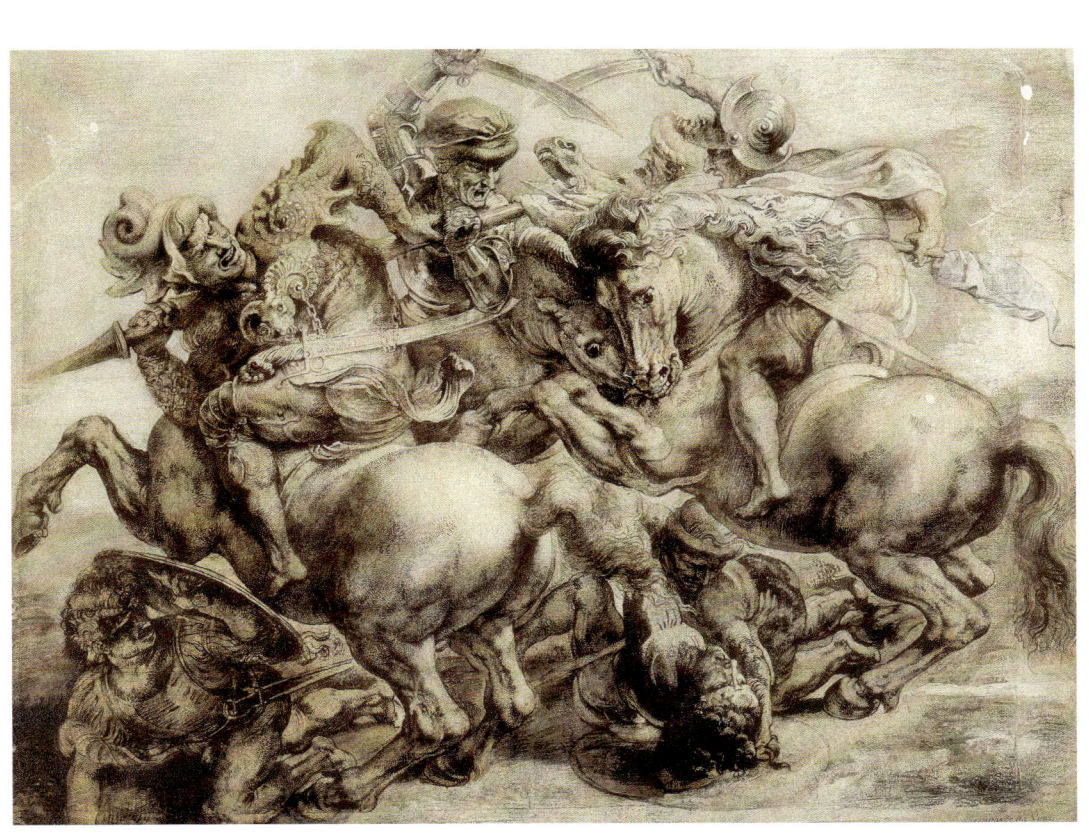

Virgin and Child with St Anne (c. 1503–19)

Oil on poplar
168 × 113 cm
Musée du Louvre, Paris

In this painting, the Virgin Mary and infant Christ are joined by Mary's mother, St Anne. Inventive as this composition is, the painting elicits respect rather than warmth. Raphael emulated Leonardo's Holy Family pyramidal compositions, adding a restrained sweetness. This painting lacks the intimacy of the *Madonna of the Yarnwinder* (page 85). Art historian, Kenneth Clark lamented Leonardo's increasing tendency to regularise features of these figures, "losing thereby something of the freshness and humanity".

Details of stones and botany come from the artist's lengthy studies of petrology and fossils. At the time he painted this, Leonardo went on excursions specifically to view fossils in situ near Rome. The landscape is invented but includes features and effects that he had recorded in writing and drawing.

The use of poplar suggests *Virgin and Child with St Anne* was started in Leonardo's second Florentine period; its style—and indirect documentary evidence—indicates it was worked on for the rest of his life. At the time of his death this painting remained incomplete, mainly in the foreground. Flatness of the Virgin Mary's blue robe is due to pigment deterioration rather than a lack of finish. Excessive restoration has removed some of Leonardo's *chiaroscuro* glazes, thereby reducing the volumetric shading of the Virgin's face.

In early October 1517 Antonio de Beatis visited Leonardo's studio in Cloux, with his master the Cardinal of Aragon. "[Leonardo] showed His Lordship three pictures, one of a certain Florentine lady, done from life at the instigation of the late Magnifico Giuliano de' Medici, another of the young St John the Baptist, and another of the Madonna and Child placed on the lap of St Anne: all quite perfect. However, we cannot expect any more great work from him, since he is now somewhat paralysed in his right hand. He has trained up a Milanese pupil who works well. And while Master Leonardo can no longer colour with such sweetness as he used to, he is none the less able to do drawings and to teach others." Beatis seems to be in error. The left-handed artist was unlikely to have been impaired by paralysis to his right side.

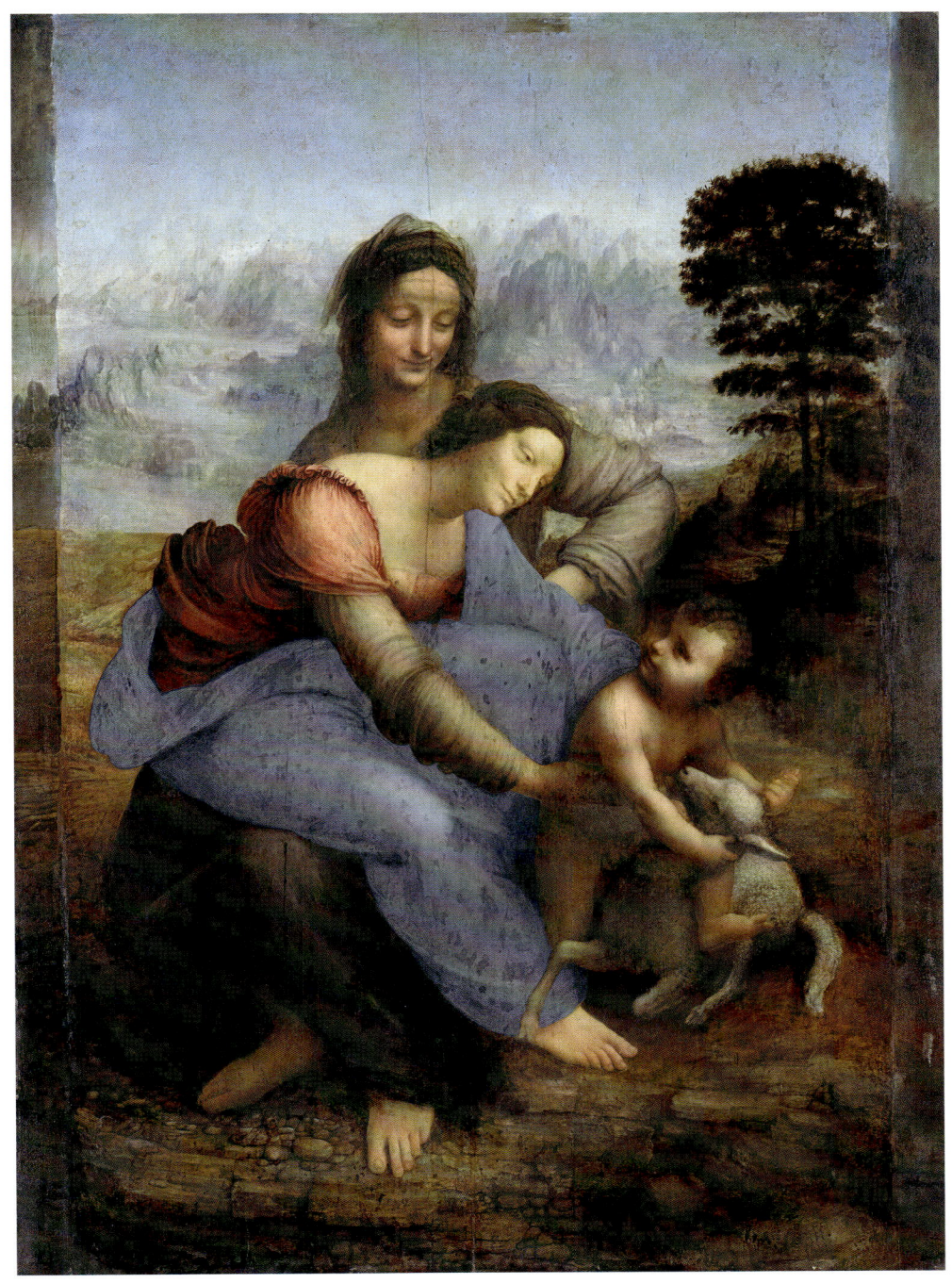

The Virgin and Child with Saint Anne and the Infant Saint John the Baptist (The Burlington House Cartoon) (c. 1506–8)

Charcoal with white chalk on paper, mounted on canvas
141.5 × 104.6 cm
The National Gallery, London

In this drawing the Christ Child is accompanied by his mother Mary, grandmother Anne and the infant St John the Baptist. It is one of Leonardo's strangest pictures, suffused with mystery, ambiguous in mood and form. The bodies seem permeable, with limbs not clearly fixed in place or even attached to bodies. Alternative gestures and contours make this large drawing more of a giant thumbnail sketch than a cartoon made to provide outlines for painting. It has been heavily worked but certain parts (St Anne's hand, the feet) are merely outlined. The age and sex of St Anne have been rendered hard to read. The proclivity to make figures ambiguous would reach its culmination in *St John* (page 95).

Considering the expense and trouble expended to compose the surface (multiple sheets of paper pasted together) and the time spent drawing, it is appropriate to ask for what purpose this drawing was made? It must have been a demonstration of Leonardo's ideas and ability and the artist no doubt considered it sufficient in itself. Painters sometimes produced cartoons specifically for transfer of composition outlines, without shading or detail. We have no record of Leonardo's studio working in that way.

This drawing once belonged to the Royal Academy, London, the premises of which was Burlington House, where this drawing was used as a teaching aid. This is one of three extant cartoons by Leonardo. The others are the *Portrait of a Lady in Profile* (page 83) and the head of the infant St John from the first *The Virgin of the Rocks* (page 57). We have reports of a cartoon of the holy family, including a lamb, from around 1500, but this is both a separate design and stylistically later. Other cartoons have since disappeared.

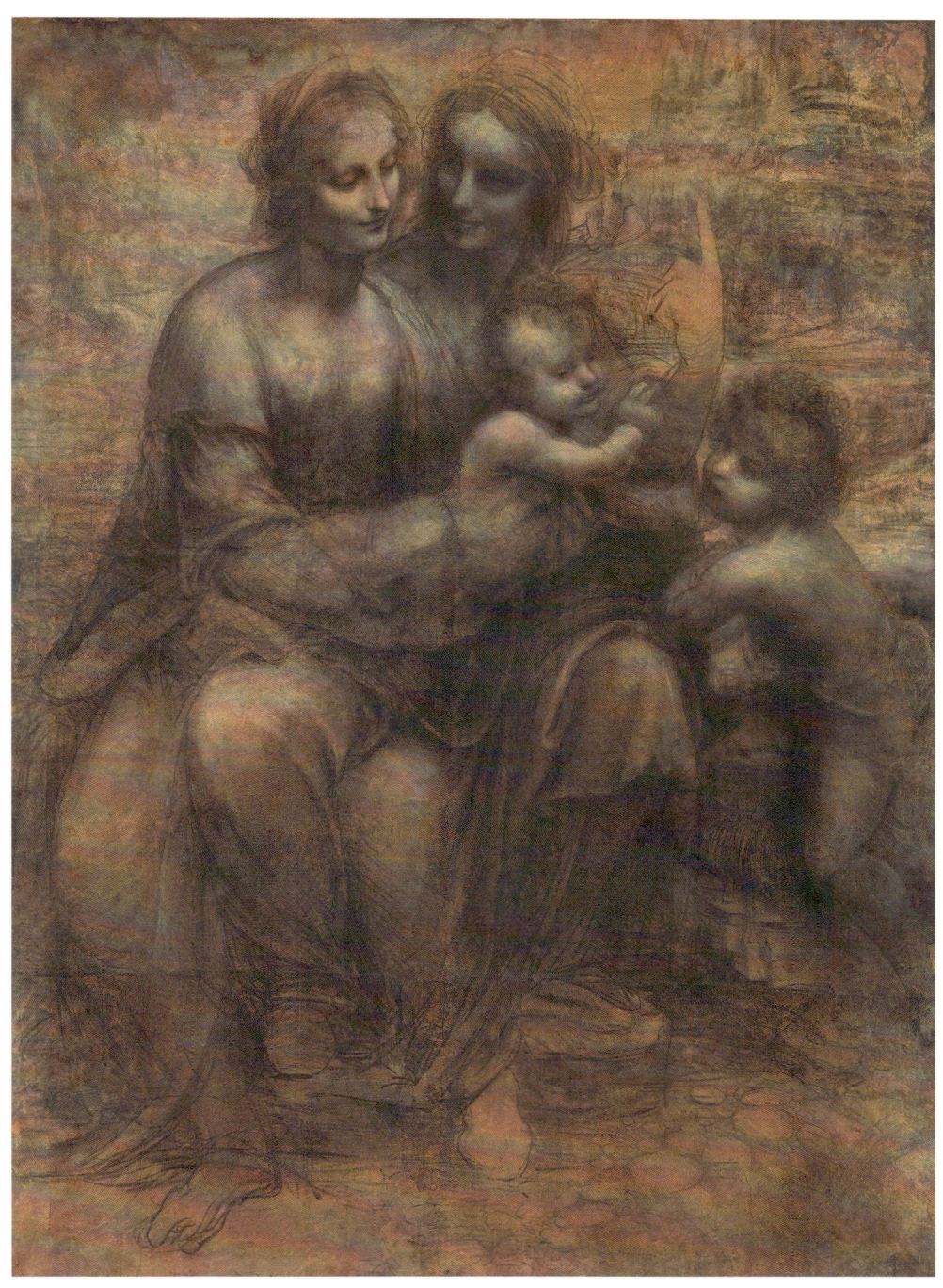

Storm over a Valley (c. 1506–1510)

Red chalk on paper
20 × 15 cm
Royal Library, Windsor

In a sequence of drawings from the 1510s, Leonardo executed black-chalk drawings of deluges destroying mountains and buildings. In these we have the impression of Leonardo wrestling with the catastrophe of natural forces and—by extension—death. This drawing is much more naturalistic in character, but it is a precursor to those apocalyptic visions. If this view of a landscape is factual, no one has yet been able to identify its location. Literal or not, it is a view of the Alps. The tops of cumulonimbus clouds become analogous to the mountain peaks which they surround. It relates to an entry in the notebooks: "[Monte Rosa?] lifts itself so great a height as almost to pass above all the clouds; and snow seldom falls there, but only hail in summer when the clouds are at their greatest height". Leonardo produced some tiny, exquisite views of snowclad mountains in the Alps, made using red and white chalks on tinted paper and executed during rest stops whilst travelling.

This drawing was made at a time when Leonardo was studying hydrodynamics, which fed into related studies of the role of airflow in flight dynamics, the flow of blood in the cardiovascular system and the action of water in the erosion of stone. The natural cycles of evaporation, cloud formation, precipitation and the movement of water through rivers to the sea was a process observed by Leonardo and which he compared to other natural cycles. He was forever delving deeply and noting analogies never previously recorded. "Motion is the principle of all life", he concluded.

Leonardo's investigation of the natural world led him to the study of fossils. About the fossilised remains of a whale Leonardo wrote: "O powerful and once-living instrument of formative nature, thy great strength not availing thee thou must needs abandon life to obey the law which God and time gave to creative nature.... Oh, how many a time the terrified shoal of dolphins and big tunny fish were seen to flee before thy insensate fury". For Leonardo, observable phenomena such as rainfall and wind shaped the earth, and everything around him was in the vast process of change, however infinitesimally slowly. In the form of fossils, animals could take on the durability of stone, only to be ultimately exposed to the elements and reduced to dust.

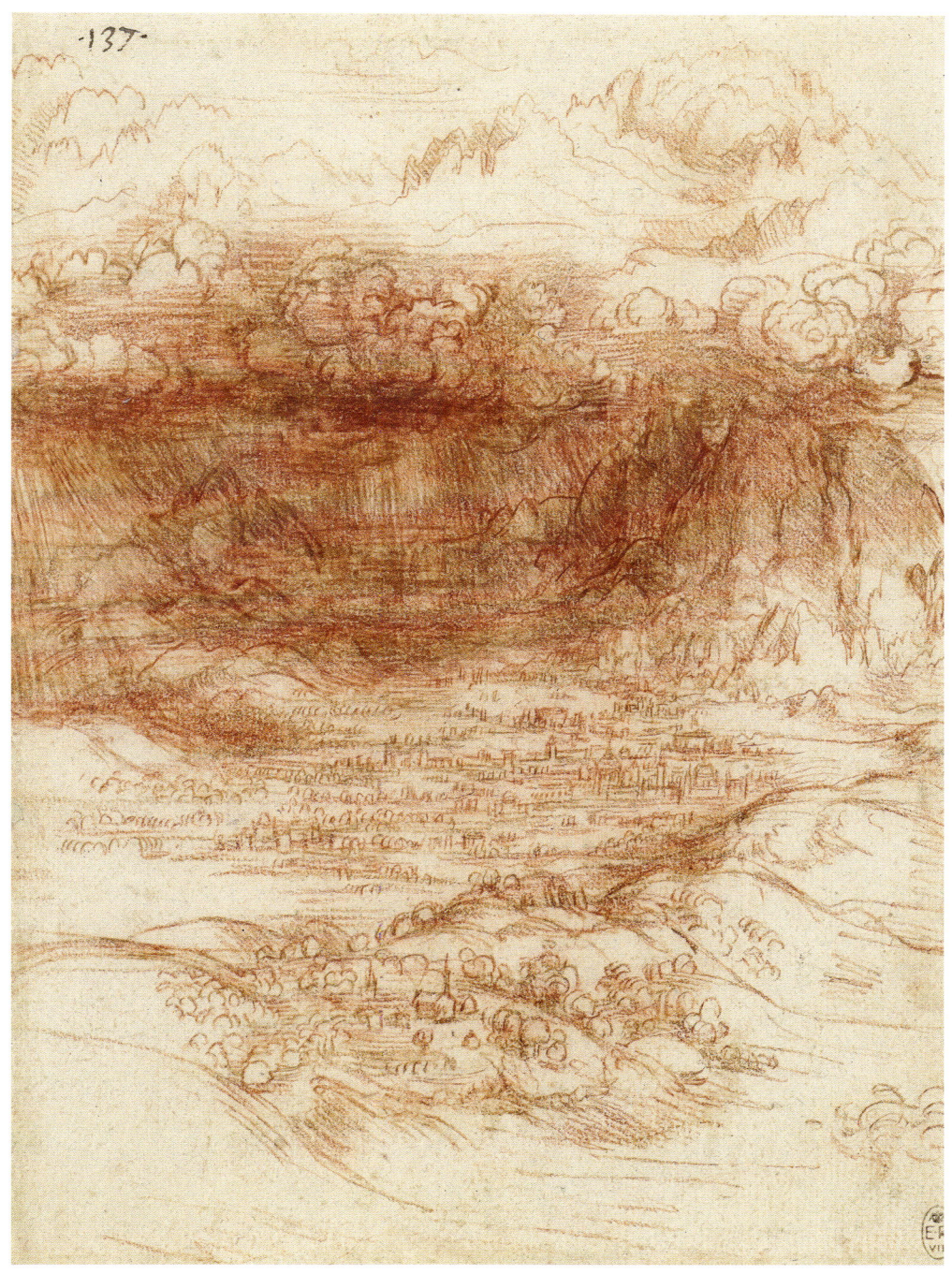

Christ as Salvator Mundi (c. 1499–1507)

Studio of Leonardo da Vinci (?)
Oil on walnut
65.5 × 45.1 cm
Private collection

Christ is depicted as saviour of the world (*salvator mundi*), holding a calcite crystal orb in his left hand and offering a gesture of benediction with his right. The orb represents the temporal realm; the benediction is a holy blessing and a promise of salvation. The black background had become Leonardo's preferred method of heightening spiritual intensity.

The composition of Leonardo's *Salvator Mundi* was widely copied throughout the sixteenth century and reproduced in a 1650 engraving by Wenceslaus Hollar. The design is described as Leonardo's, whether or not transmission is through an autograph painting. Interestingly, this painter has neglected the distorted refraction of light observed through clear crystal, something that Leonardo—an expert in optics—had observed firsthand.

Is this by Leonardo? Walter Isaacson and Martin Kemp believe it to be authentic; Jacques Franck, Carmen Bambach and Frank Zöllner doubt it; Charles Hope rejects it; Brian Sewell found it impossible to decide due to its condition. This picture was heavily repainted before 1900, leading to its dismissal by historians. Extensive campaigns of restoration—at least two—in the last twenty years have noticeably altered its appearance. What might have been the original artist's handiwork is practically indecipherable, making a decision on its authenticity moot. In my view, this painting is old, possibly originating from Leonardo's studio, but I cannot see any evidence of paintwork by Leonardo himself. *Salvator Mundi* was sold by Christie's, New York on 15 November 2017 for $450.3 million. It reportedly passed into the possession of Mohammed bin Salman, who subsequently promised to exhibit it at a museum in Abu Dhabi.

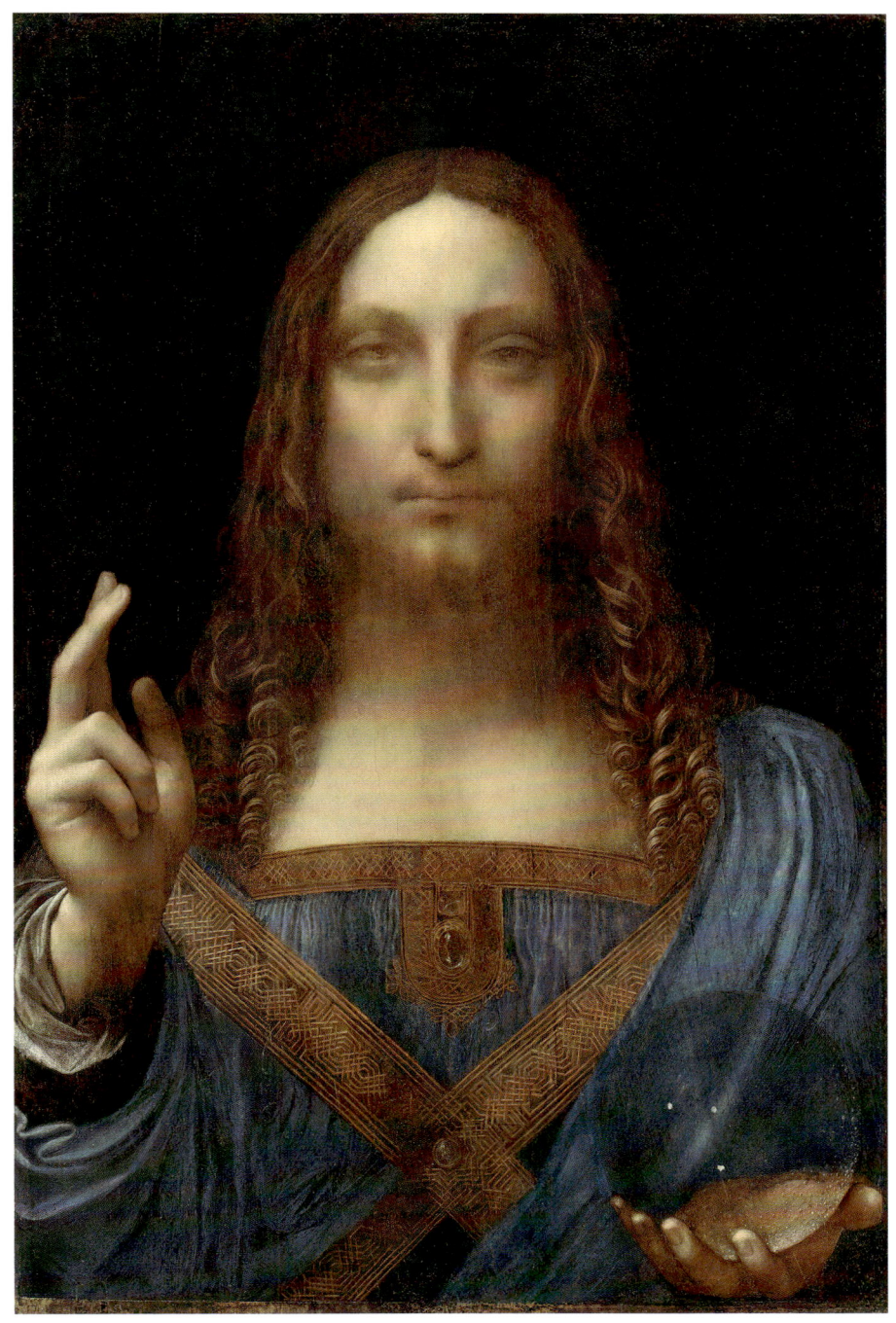

The Muscles of the Shoulder and Arm and the Bones of the Foot (c. 1510/11)

Pen and ink with wash over chalk on paper
28.9 × 20.1 cm
Royal Library, Windsor

"This old man, a few hours before his death, told me that he had lived one hundred years and that he was conscious of no bodily failure other than feebleness. And thus sitting on a bed in the hospital of S. Maria Nuova, without any movement or sign of distress, he passed from this life. And I made an anatomy to see the cause of a death so sweet." Leonardo's subsequent investigation comprises the first ever clinical diagnosis of coronary atherosclerosis. These drawings depict another subject, describing the myology of the shoulder, neck and chest of an elderly man. Questioned late in life, Leonardo claimed to have dissected over thirty cadavers in the course of his anatomical studies. He travelled to Padua for the purpose of performing or observing dissections at the university. As the practice of human dissection—on church or university premises—was strictly regulated by the Church, Leonardo needed permission to perform dissections. Dissection itself was considered highly disreputable, adjacent to witchcraft. In 1564 pioneer anatomist Vesalius would be condemned to death for dissection, a sentence that would be commuted to pilgrimage. It seems that Leonardo performed unsanctioned dissections; he tells of staying with bodies overnight, perhaps in his own rooms. In Rome, Leonardo wrote that assistants assigned to him disrupted his work and he complained about being distracted and spied upon. Eventually, he would lose his privileges to have access to bodies, which effectively terminated his studies. He would never resume them. Leonardo did have sufficient drawings to assemble illustrations for a treatise on anatomy but—ever the perfectionist—he delayed completion. Although other artists (including Michelangelo) also drew dissections, Leonardo went well beyond the unclothed and flayed body with which artists familiarised themselves. He studied the nerves, digestive system, brain, genito-urinary system and embryology (page 101) in a ceaseless attempt to understand all human biology.

The anatomical and mechanical drawings are models of clarity and logic. The exploded view, sequential rotated position and cross-section allow flat images to explicate complex dense structures. Combination of diagrammatic linear description and volumetric shading provide an artificial balance that make his drawings clearly comprehensible. These aspects would provide the template for all future technical illustrations and continue to be applied today.

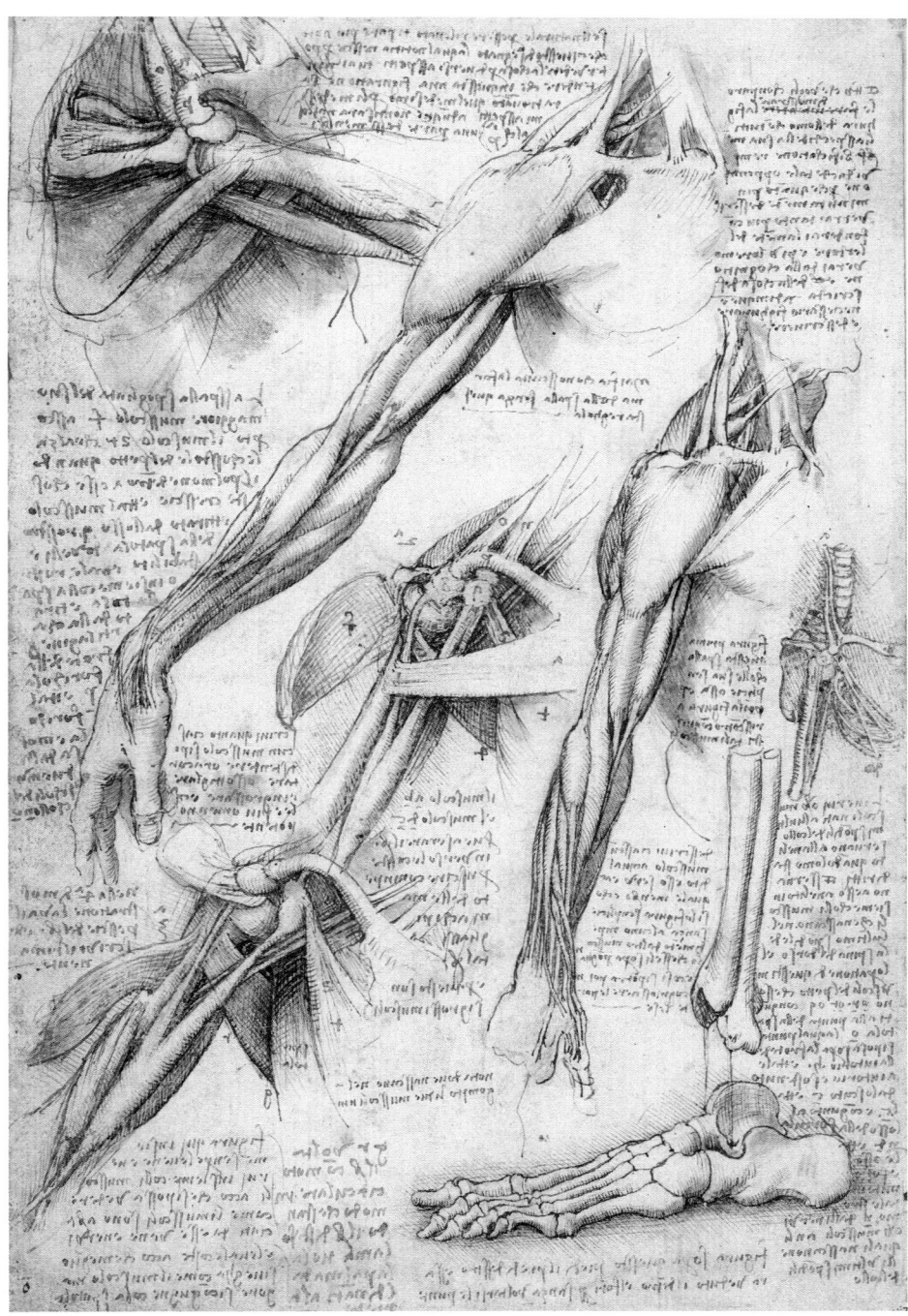

Foetus in the Womb (c. 1510–2)

Pen and ink with wash over black and red chalk on paper
30.4 × 22 cm
Royal Library, Windsor

Part of the text reads, "The heart of this child does not beat nor does it breathe because it continually lies in water. If it breathed it would drown and breathing is not necessary because [it is] vivified and nourished by the life and food of the mother . . .. One and the same soul governs these two bodies". Leonardo was unaware of the foetal heartbeat, there being no current technology able to detect this.

The artist's observations are not based on the embryo in situ. Instead they are deduced from the study of a stillborn baby, which he has drawn with characteristic care and accuracy. He dissected an infant to compare its anatomy to that of an adult.

Leonardo did commit errors due to faulty deductions. The cadavers available for dissection in this time were usually those of executed criminals; consequently, there were fewer female bodies available for inspection. Leonardo resorted to comparative mammalian anatomy, such as when he dissected a cow uterus to investigate the reproductive system of women. He made inferences that were incorrect, something he would have spotted had his career as an anatomist not ended just a few years after this drawing had been made.

The diagrams on the right are of the placental cotyledons, which process blood within the placenta. These drawings are based on the dissections of a cow placenta and differ from human biology, which Leonardo would have recognised had he had access to a human sample.

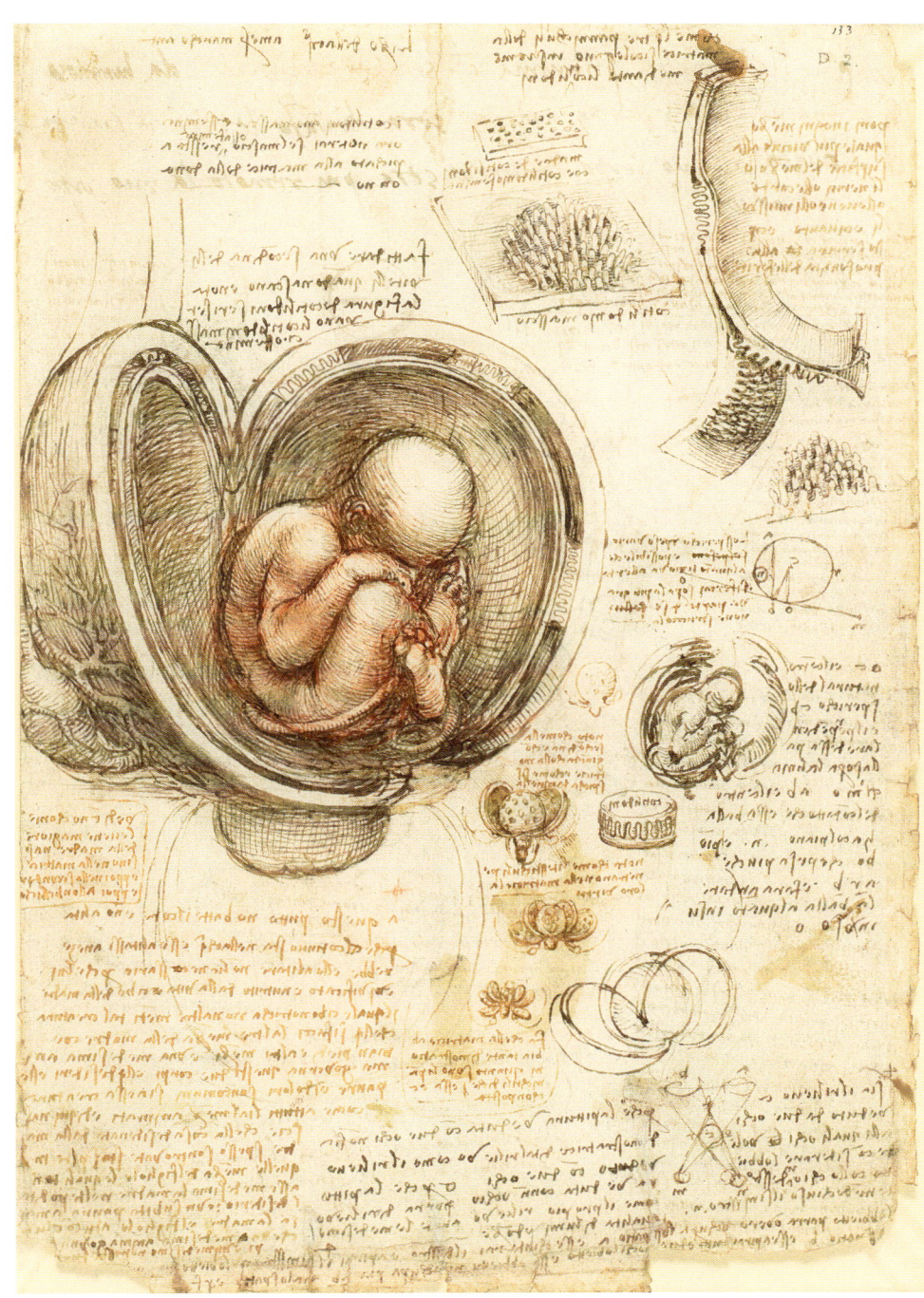

Head of a Bearded Man (Self-portrait?)
(c. 1510–5)

Red chalk on paper
33.3 × 21.5 cm
Biblioteca Reale, Turin

We have a craving to see the face of the artist and read the physiognomy and bearing of a creator who sees so acutely. We wish to gaze into the master's eyes and to comprehend him in psychological terms. By extension, we believe we shall come to know more about ourselves and what it is to be human. There are no uncontested self-portraits in Leonardo's corpus, painted or drawn. The young soldier in the *Adoration* (page 55) and *Vitruvian Man* (page 69) have both been thought to be possible likenesses of the painter. Is this drawing a self-portrait of the elderly artist? The subject seems to emanate the gravity and dignity of Leonardo in old age. It resembles the portrait of Plato from Raphael's *School of Athens* (1509–1511), which tradition holds that it is a depiction of Leonardo. If this drawing dates from his Roman period or before (as some scholars suggest), Leonardo would have been aged about 60, so what are we to make of his elderly appearance? Those who met him in his last decade judged him older than he was and in poor health. Yet, at around this time, a portrait made by one of the master's assistants, probably Melzi (page 2), shows a similar looking but noticeably younger Leonardo. It has been suggested that this studio portrait (in Windsor) is an idealised version of the master, perhaps produced shortly after his death. The Windsor portrait was used as the basis for the portrait in Vasari's biography of Leonardo.

In this drawing is Leonardo using his anatomical knowledge and skill in caricature to depict himself as a very venerable man? If so, that would make this Turin portrait, in effect, Leonardo's experiment in projection of a future self.

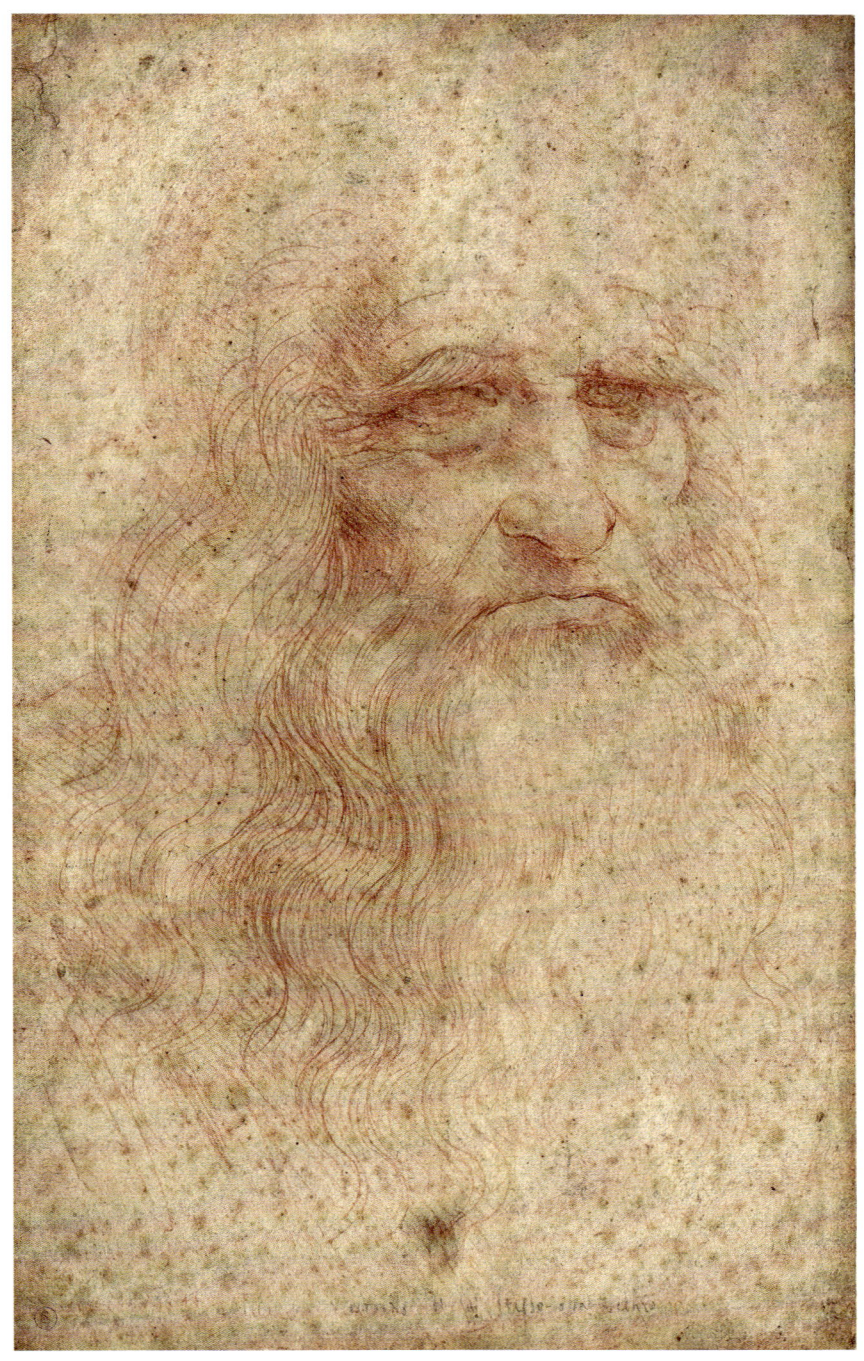

St John the Baptist (c. 1513–6)

Oil on walnut
72.9 × 56.3 cm
Musée du Louvre, Paris

Along with the *Mona Lisa* (page 87) and *Virgin and Child with St Anne* (page 91), this painting was brought to France by Leonardo when he arrived in 1516. St John the Baptist is depicted in the darkness of his cave dwelling. His left hand indicates himself as a prophet; more prominently, with his other hand, he refers to the divine origin of the messiah who is to follow him. The shading renders the saint insubstantial. St John seems not so much to inhabit the darkness as to be a part of it.

Leonardo declared that there are no lines in nature, only volumes. In pictorial terms, this entails the description of forms through shadow, a technique called *chiaroscuro* (It: light-dark). This is linked to *sfumato* (It: to disperse like smoke), which is the softening of forms using blurring. In oil painting these ends are achieved by applying delicate semi-transparent glazes that modulate colour and tone. These techniques reach their ultimate expression in *St John*, which is the product of prolonged meditation and drawn-out execution—hallmarks of Leonardo's late period.

This painting, which is considered to be Leonardo's final one, has drawn forceful responses from viewers. Many have found the painting repulsive, with the figure—supposedly based upon Salaì—attracting negative comment. Aspersions have been cast on the physique, judging it to be androgynous and overweight. Jules Michelet wrote, "This canvas [sic] attracts me, overwhelms me, absorbs me; I go toward it in spite of myself, like the bird toward the snake". Bernard Berenson was repulsed by *St John*.

Viewing Leonardo's late paintings, we can get an unsettling sensation of singularity. The Leonardo face of the late period—with its prominent straight, "Greek" nose, rounded chin and heavy drooping eyelids—is not derived from observation but has become a persistent type. One cannot tell mother from daughter, man from woman, human from divine. The artist who once declared, "A painter who takes no account of these varieties [among men] always makes his figures on one pattern so that they might all be taken for brothers", had become mannered. Mona Lisa's knowing smile has been superseded by St John's ambiguous smirk.

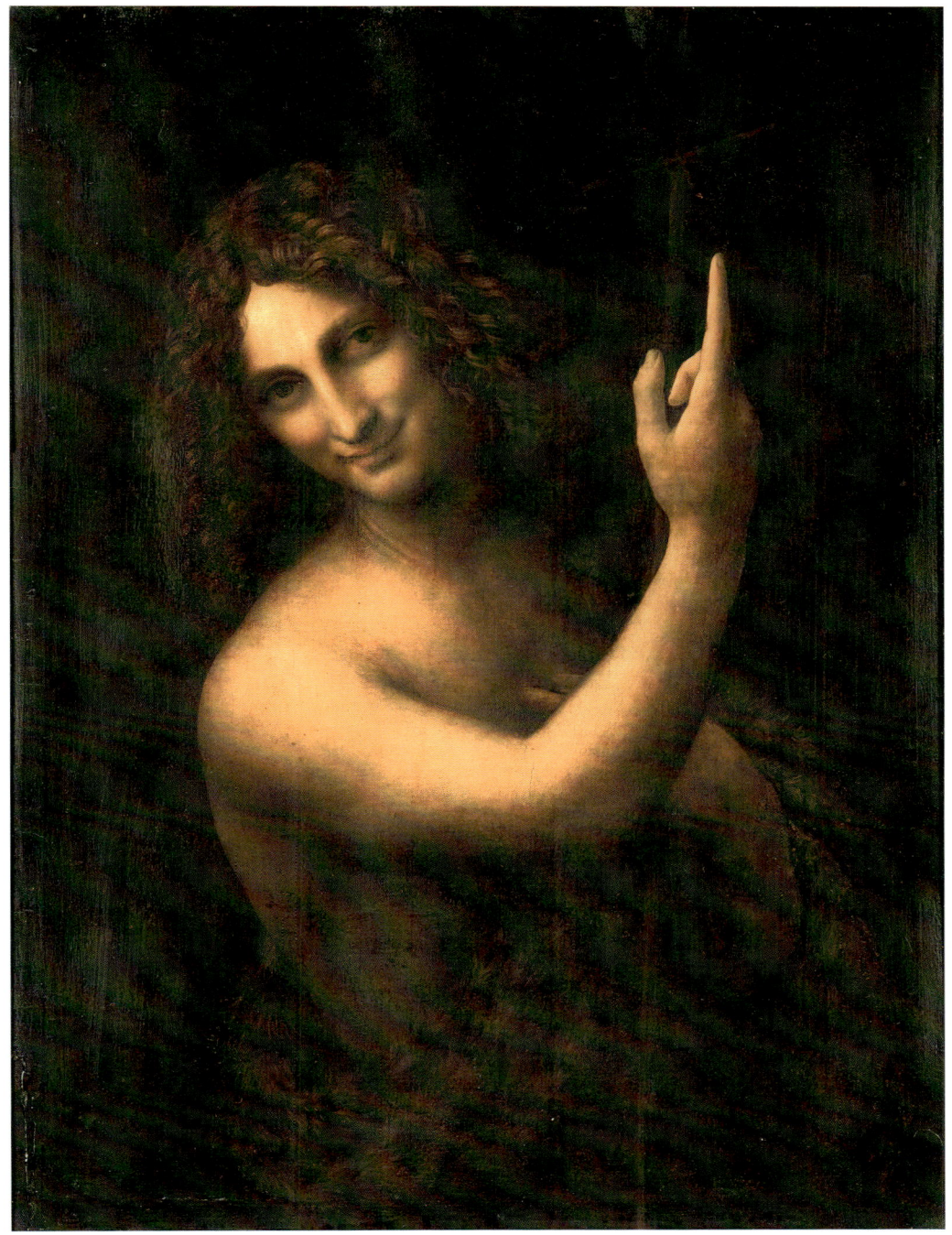

St John the Baptist in the Wilderness
(with the Attributes of Bacchus) (c. 1513–9)

Studio of Leonardo da Vinci
Oil on walnut, transferred to canvas
177 × 115 cm
Musée du Louvre, Paris

Current scholarly consensus is that—even if the original composition may be the master's—Leonardo's assistants executed this painting. It is closely related to the *St John* (page 105). As that painting is more highly regarded than this one, *St John* is dated earlier and the Bacchus-St John has been relegated to the status of a later variant. However, it has been suggested that due to a (presumed) narrowing of focus and intensifying of emotion in Leonardo's last years, the reverse might be the case, with the previous *St John* being a concentrated distillation of this more expansive composition. Disappointment with this work has made it an anticlimactic end to chronological accounts of Leonardo's achievements.

This painting originally depicted St John the Baptist in the wilderness; the attributes of Bacchus, the Greek god of wine, are a leopard (or panther) skin and a vine-leaf crown which were added later. The cross that the figure held was turned into a staff. A layer of lead-white disrupts X-rays, which means it is very difficult to determine when changes were made to the painting and whether they were made in Leonardo's studio. In the original composition, the right hand indicated the (now lost) cross symbol of Christ as the coming redeemer of mankind, the left index finger pointed downwards to hell, destiny for those who refuse Christ. Regardless of the motive for the transformation into Bacchus, these alterations render the figure's gestures meaningless. Recent cleaning has revealed a bright sky and landscape, once obscured under discoloured varnish. Examination showed no part painted with Leonardo's ability. Leonardo's practice is complicated because it sometimes inverts the traditional division of labour, where the master paints the most important figures, and assistants do the backgrounds and minor details.

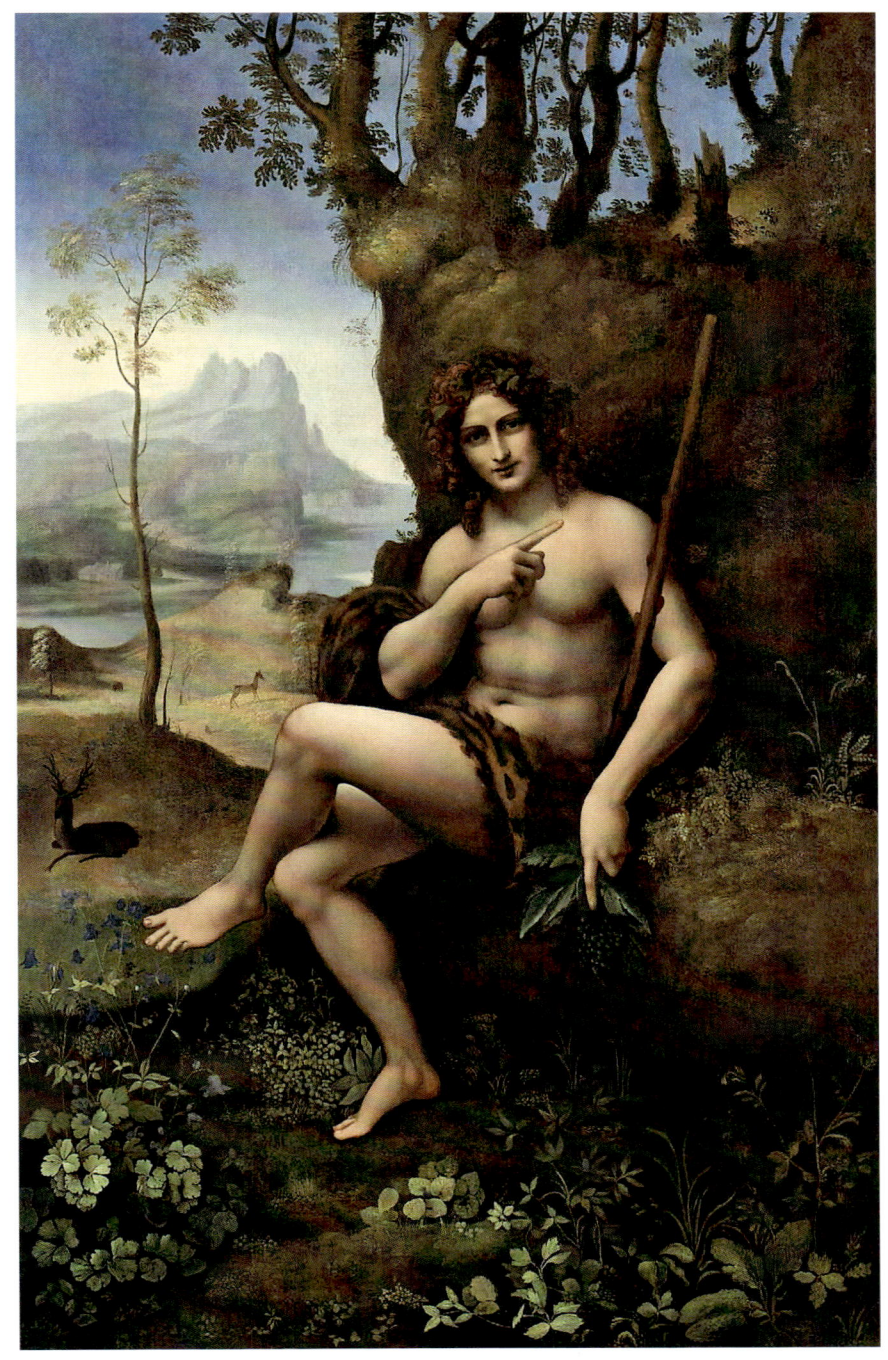

Allegory with a Wolf and Eagle
(c. 1508–10? or c. 1515/6?)

Red chalk on brown–grey paper
17 × 28 cm
Royal Library, Windsor

Dating from Leonardo's Roman period, this fantasy shows a wolf—with some overtones of a bull and bear—guiding a boat with a tree for a mast, orientating himself towards a globe surmounted by a crowned eagle. It is a wonderful piece of invention, crackling with energy and luxuriating in the sensuous medium of chalk on paper.

Notebooks reveal that Leonardo had a fondness for wordplay. He was forever writing puns and riddles; he played with words, images and symbols. In a milieu where heraldry was deployed to communicate in ways profound and witty, Leonardo was alive to the power of allegories. His library contained Aesop's *Fables* and comic epics; he turned his hand to writing short parables, invented incidents and imagined travelogues. Intertwining real and unreal to present deeper truths came as naturally to Leonardo as his scientific materialism.

Among the artist's papers we find a number of allegorical drawings mixing heraldry, prophecy and propaganda. Part of his occupation as a courtier was to entertain and ennoble patrons. Leonardo's allegories are difficult to interpret because—unlike the presentation-drawing allegories of Michelangelo—we do not know to whom these allegories are addressed, or indeed if they were made for anyone other than Leonardo himself.

This drawing is considered political in character. Kemp suggests that it depicts the pope (wolf) steering the church (ship) towards King François I (crowned eagle), foreshadowing a potential alignment between the Catholic Church and the monarch. If it was made during Leonardo's Roman period to curry favour with the French king, it is peculiar that it never entered his collection. It stayed with Leonardo until his death.

It is impossible to pin down the exact symbolism of this allegory. Like many of the products of Leonardo's mind, it remains elusive, intriguing and ultimately unknowable, drawing us in to Leonardo's characteristic playful wit, dazzling skill and peerless ingenuity.

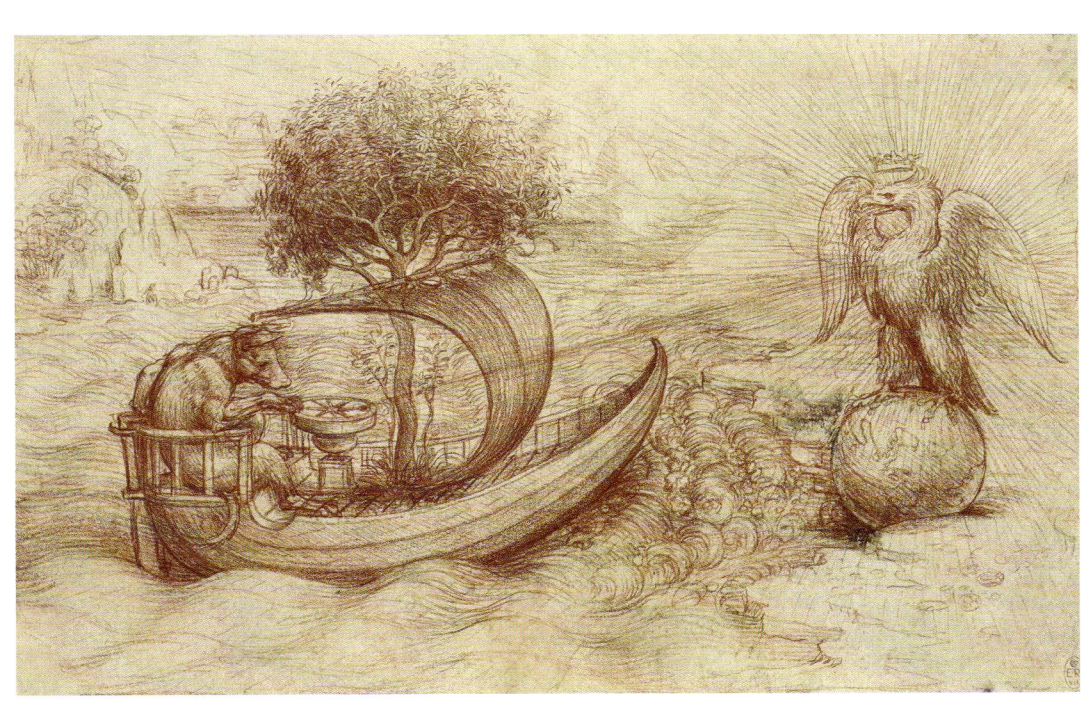

FURTHER READING

Bedini *et al*, Silvio A., *The Unknown Leonardo*, London, 1974

Bramly, Serge, *Leonardo: The Artist and the Man*, London, 1991

Butterfield, Andrew (ed.), *Verrocchio: Sculptor and Painter of Renaissance Florence*, Washington DC, 2021

Campbell, Stephen J., *Leonardo da Vinci: An Untraceable Life*, London, 2025

Kemp, Martin, and Roberts, Jane, *Leonardo da Vinci*, London, 1989

Kemp, Martin, *Leonardo da Vinci: Marvellous Works of Nature and Man*, Oxford, 1981/2006

King, Ross, *Leonardo and the Last Supper*, London, 2012

Leonardo on the Human Body, New York, 1952

Marani, Pietro C., and Fiorio, Maria Testa (eds.), *Leonardo da Vinci: The Design of the World*, Milan, 2015

Nicholl, Charles, *Leonardo da Vinci: The Flights of the Mind*, London, 2005

Popham, A.E., *The Drawings of Leonardo da Vinci*, London, 1946

Richter, Irma A. (ed.), *The Notebooks of Leonardo da Vinci*, Oxford, 2018

Syson, Luke (ed.), *Leonardo da Vinci: Painter at the Court of Milan*, London, 2011

Vasari, Giorgio, *Lives of the Artists*, Florence, 1550/1568

Zöllner, Frank, *Leonardo: The Complete Paintings and Drawings*, Munich, 2019

PHOTO CREDITS